REDEMPTION OF A COUNTERSPY

A TRUE STORY OF HOW EVIL ALMOST TOOK THE LIFE OF A U.S. GOVERNMENT AGENT

SAMMY VILLELA

Copyright © 2022 by Sammy Villela

All rights reserved.

No part of this book may be reproduced in any form or by any electronic or mechanical means, including information storage and retrieval systems, without written permission from the author, except for the use of brief quotations in a book review.

❦ Created with Vellum

CONTENTS

Foreword — vii
CEO, Project Healing Heroes

Acknowledgments — xi
Introduction — xiii

Prologue — 1

PART ONE
IN THE BEGINNING

Chapter 1 — 9
THE ARNET BENSON

Chapter 2 — 19
CHANGING THE TRAJECTORY

Chapter 3 — 29
URBAN JUNGLE

Chapter 4 — 39
A SOLDIER

PART TWO
SLIPPING INTO DARKNESS

Chapter 5 — 53
THE SHEEP DOG

Chapter 6 — 65
GOD, WHERE ARE YOU?

Chapter 7 — 75
THE UNIMAGINABLE

PART THREE
FOUND PEOPLE WHO FIND PEOPLE

Chapter 8   87
THE POWER OF ONE

Chapter 9   99
SHOOTING STARS

Chapter 10   111
TRIAD OF TRANSFORMATION

PART FOUR
SAVED PEOPLE WHO SERVE PEOPLE

Chapter 11   125
MY DIRTY TOWEL

Chapter 12   135
WORLDVIEW

Chapter 13   149
TIO SAM MINISTRIES

Epilogue   159

About the Author   163
About the Author continued   165
Photo Album   167

*This book is dedicated to the men and women on active duty, our military veterans, and our first responders who are no longer with us today because the demons inside the darkest places of their hearts whispered despair, hopelessness, and depression into their minds, eventually causing them to take their own lives.
Moreover, to those still with us, continuously battling the invisible wounds of war and trauma, may you find the peace and grace of God and never give up the good fight.*

FOREWORD
LT COL DR. DAVID F. THARP
CEO, PROJECT HEALING HEROES

Most Americans are passionately in pursuit of the American Dream. They literally dream of a better life for themselves and their family. To have a good paying job, a house in the suburbs, manicured lawn, great health care, financial stability, and ultimately, an enjoyable and fulfilling retirement. So much so, that their peaceful rest may even include dreams of living on an island, drinking their favorite beverage, sand in their toes, all while waves crash the beach as they watch the sun, quietly descend and fade away into a serene, picturesque sunset.

The reason most Americans can enjoy their dreams about the American Dream is unquestionably correlated to the cost of freedom, paid for by men like Sammy Villela. To be a soldier, a warrior, a counterspy comes at a high price. And instead of enjoying these same peaceful dreams, they get the pleasure of reliving painful memories, death and images of what they have experienced on sometimes a nightly basis. So much so that even the thought of going to sleep is frightening.

Watching evil exert its will over humanity is almost

indescribable, let alone unforgettable once you have witnessed it with your own eyes. Reading the stories that Sammy is able to talk about, makes one wonder about the stories that he cannot share, for reasons of national security or because they are simply too painful to relive. If the price of freedom means to go on living when others have died, the "blessings" bestowed upon them include insomnia, drugs, alcohol abuse, nightmares, night terrors, survivor guilt, moral injury and questioning the existence of God, all while being told "Thank you for your service".

It is impossible to witness and experience evil up close and personal without it taking a toll on the mind, body and soul. And yet that is and always will be, the price of American freedom.

Sammy shed's new light onto David Grossman's book entitled, "On Combat". In this book Grossman places people into one of three categories: the sheep, the wolf or the sheep dog. The average American with their dreams, sheepishly at times, don't even know or understand the sheep dog (Sammy's role) and what he does for them. As sheep, they are grateful for such men and women who do things like espionage for our country, but it is not a life for them or their children. They are much too important to ever join the military or do something of the sort. It is after all, a way of escape for those less fortunate, and well, they are "blessed". Instead of living a life of service and sacrifice, they are contemplating which fraternity or sorority to pledge, their riches to be had and building a network that they can use to their advantage.

Then there are the wolves. The tyrants of this world who justify horrendous acts of evil. They choose to listen instead to evil and do its will. They seek to devour anyone who gets in their way. And the atrocities they leave behind are permanently etched into the hearts and minds of those who try to stop them.

FOREWORD

Sheep dogs are very well trained. One such example is General, Norman Schwarzkopf. When asked if there should be forgiveness toward the people who have harbored and abetted terrorists who perpetrated the 9/11 attacks on America, he responded, "I believe that forgiving them is God's function. Our job is simply to arrange the meeting". Sheep dogs are very good at arranging meetings.

Sammy brings in a fourth actor, the shepherd that Grossman did not. And the shepherd is, as we say, the game changer. He is the ultimate overwatch. How could He not be when He is omniscient, omnipotent and omnipresent?

Welcome to Sammy's world. Sammy, like Schwarzkopf, is a sheep dog. A very good one at that! In order to defeat evil, one must know the tactics of the wolf so as to defeat him. But to know them to that extent, they have no choice but to get up close and personal. This comes at a significant, personal risk. For some, the cost is the ultimate sacrifice and a price that can truly never be paid. These are the men and women who have stood their ground even while positioned directly in the line of fire against those hell bent on doing evil in this world. They live in the crosshairs of those who seek to kill and destroy. The sheep dogs are constantly on watch. They get very little sleep because they are constantly vigilant and "on guard", they stand firm and they do not waiver.

These are the exact qualities that I have experienced and know first-hand of my dear friend, Sammy Villela. Sammy would be the first to say that he has fought many demons, on many fronts. From PTSD to Panama. And yet you will not find a more kind, compassionate, fun-loving, hulk of a man that you would trust to put a Band-Aid on your child after they fell off a swing, or be the first to connect on a swing at those who are the evil actors in this world. Except the consequences in this life is that there are no "actors" and Sammy isn't playing. When we talk about someone having your six, Sammy not only has it, he has your 3, 9 and 12 as well.

It is true, the American dream is a blessing to be had. But do not kid yourself. Those wonderful, peaceful dreams are bought and paid for by men like Sammy Villela. They are, the reason you can sleep peacefully at night and dream the American Dream.

ACKNOWLEDGMENTS

First and foremost, I want to thank God for blessing me with such an abundant life! I acknowledge that all of my life experiences, good and bad, have made me the person I am today, and for the purpose God created me for.

To my lovely wife, Tricia. Thank you for sticking by me through thick and thin, in sickness and in health. I don't deserve you, but here you remain. You are my rock, my true north and I love you with all of my being.

To my awesome sons, Victor, Jesse, Alex, and Adam, as well as my daughter-in-law, Samantha, and my grandkids, Valentino and Viviana. Thank you all for loving me and for never giving up on me. You continue to make this life worth living, and I love you all beyond words.

To my parents, Bobby and Gina, thank you for being the best, most loving parents a kid could ever ask for. You are both excellent examples of what good parents look like. I will always love you dearly.

To Rachael DeBoy, thank you for being receptive and obedient to God . . . and thereby saving my life. I love you so much, more than you'll probably ever know. You are forever my little sister and I, forever your servant.

To Danette Blair, thank you for stepping into my life and

making me fall in love with getting my towel dirty! I love you and hope we never stop getting our towels dirty together!

Finally, to my tribe! There are too many of you to name, but you know who you are! May God continue to bless you and yours, I love you all!

INTRODUCTION

Have you ever wondered what it takes to break someone to the point they are willing to take their own life? Ever wondered what it is like to return home from a war zone after experiencing the worst in humanity? Or wondered how anyone can overcome challenges related to Post Traumatic Stress Disorder without doctors, therapists, or medicine? Do you know what it is like to experience the love of Jesus Christ even when you have turned your back on Him? Well then, this book will answer all those questions in detail. Witnessing man's inhumanity toward man my entire life caused me to lose my faith in God, and in doing so, I allowed the enemy to close in on me. As he cut me off mentally from loved ones, I experienced some of the darkest years of my life as a result. I became a fake person to my family, friends, and co-workers. Because I did not want any of them to know, especially my mother, that I had lost my faith in God. Not being your true, authentic self takes its toll on your mind, body, and soul. This is why intelligence and law enforcement agents who perform undercover work for an extended period of time are closely

INTRODUCTION

monitored by psychologists—it can be detrimental to your entire being the longer you keep up the façade. Keeping up the lie tore at my soul. And the enemy was loving every minute of it.

Having been trained as a spy catcher, I inherently ran up against fake people. People who live double lives and people who know how to hide who they really are. They know how to lie, cheat, and steal. But eventually, they all get caught. Terrorists are the same way. Some would argue that depending on where you live, terrorists are just freedom fighters. I disagree. When you intentionally target and kill innocent civilians, especially innocent women and children, you are a bad guy and need to be stopped. As a Special Agent for U.S. Army Counterintelligence, this has been my job for the past thirty-two years as of the writing of this book. It is what I have done my entire adult life, since I was eighteen years old. Overall, it has been a good ride, but with plenty of heavy and severe thunderstorms. I have met some of the best people humanity has to offer, and of course some of the worst scum of this fallen world. My only regret is not having spent a few more precious moments with my sons when they were kids.

I wrote this book for the individuals battling invisible wounds from war or other trauma. For the individuals fighting depression and/or contemplating suicide. It is also written for the spouses or caretakers of such individuals, in the hopes it gives you greater understanding of the mess that can be the mind of such people, and provide you tools you can leverage to help someone you love. It is never too late, nor are you too broken or your loved ones too broken, to begin your healing journey.

As a disclaimer, I will just say this is how I began to heal. I do acknowledge there are people out there who need professional services and medications. I chose not to go that route and was

INTRODUCTION

successful. But it doesn't mean this is the only way or that this way will work for you. However, if you are at the end of your rope and have tried everything else, what have you got to lose by trying what I outline in this book?

This book will walk you through my experiences as a child, because I need you first to understand the environment I was raised in, the violence that has accompanied me my entire life. Some of my childhood will be described without using specific names of family members out of respect for them. You will also read about some of my training and a few experiences as a counterspy. I have changed some of the tactics, techniques, and procedures for operational security purposes. If you are a CI Agent reading this book, you may think to yourself at some point while reading it, "That's not how it's done." And you will be right. That is intentional. In some cases I have changed the true names of people, in other cases instead of changing the names I have simply written "name omitted" in their place.

You will read about the darkest years of my life, and the impact they had on those around me. This is important for me that you understand so you can compare and contrast the later years, when I was saved and beyond. Being saved is the pivotal moment in this book; it is when everything changed. It is how YOU can change. It was also important for me that you get to know those people in my life who facilitated that change. My tribe, as I like to refer to them, are angels on earth and, together with my wife, are the reason I am still here. I believe they have been used mightily by God to help me understand my purpose for being here, the reason God created me.

You may notice this book is structured into four parts, similar to how the Bible is structured. The Bible starts first with creation,

INTRODUCTION

then the fall, followed by redemption, and lastly, restoration. In like fashion, my book is divided into four parts, *In the Beginning, Slipping Into Darkness, Found People Who Find People,* and *Saved People Who Serve People.* This is done as my own sort of artistic touch that gives praise to God and honors His living Word, the Gospel. The book is designed to be a quick and easy read, but host to powerful and key components to overcoming depression, suicide and PTSD, if you will simply believe. My goal with this book is to illustrate how the love of Jesus does not change and is given freely, even to a sinner like me who did not deserve it. Because good people don't go to heaven, forgiven people do. Healing from your past in this fallen world is important to your future in eternity. Like my good friend, Dr. David Tharp, Founder of Project Healing Heroes, likes to say, "It is time to stop treating wounded warriors, and start healing heroes."

I hope you enjoy my story.

PROLOGUE

> "*For the Lord God does nothing without revealing his secret to his servants the prophets.*" – Amos 3:7

0315 Hours – Somewhere in northern Iraq

EVENINGS IN IRAQ can be quite lovely. The night sky is breathtaking; the unavoidable beauty of the stars is amplified by a bright, Arabian moon that casts a spotlight on those below it. The desert in the north near the Turkish border is rather cool this time of year in September.

As we drove from our base camp at Tal Afar just after midnight, my team was quiet, everyone alone with their individual thoughts. Three of our men were in the truck behind us, and there were four more in the lead Toyota pick-up, including our local partisan and driver, Bilal, and myself. Bilal had worked with the

Special Forces here since before the war and spoke Turkish, Kurdish, Persian Farsi, Arabic, and English. He had killed insurgents in Iraq with his bare hands. But he especially liked killing Iraqi Sunnis. Under Saddam's reign, the Sunnis had slaughtered almost his entire Kurdish village northeast of Mosul and most of his family as well, all when he was only ten years old. Even so, it was his mother's death that still haunted him the most. She was raped in front of him and then beaten viciously with sticks by four of Saddam's henchmen. While she was still alive, they cut off her arms and legs and left her to bleed to death. He and his father and two brothers walked for over a month to seek refuge at the Iranian border along with a handful of survivors from his village. His older brother died along the way from illness, exhaustion, and dehydration.

Our teammates were scanning their sectors as we drove north by northwest into the desert wasteland, looking for any signs of trouble. We were on our way to link up with a man who had a brother in the United States we had nicknamed the "Bartender" because of his love of alcohol. We believed the Bartender's family could help us find a High Value Target, or HVT.

As we approached the family of the Bartender in a compound in northern Iraq, our unseen scout team conducted a radio check with me, letting me know that they could see me and had my back. They had been hiding in the vicinity of the village for days... watching, listening, and making observations, all of which were up linked to us at the base via satellite communications. Until we showed up, they had been observing the village and the Bartender's family as well as their home to make sure the family was who they said they were, and to make sure my team and I weren't walking into an ambush... I hate surprises.

A man named Jasem came out of the home to meet us as we drove up.

"Can I help you?" he asked us, rather guarded and in Arabic.

"We are friends of your relative, the Bartender in America," I said through my interpreter, Bilal. It had been what Jasem's brother (our friend, the Bartender, from the U.S.) had told him we would say when men matching our description showed up at the pre-determined date and time.

Establishing bona fides, Jasem then shook my hand with passion, and thanked us in English for coming to him. Confident the scout teams had done their homework, I walked into Jasem's home with Bilal and two of our men. The other three waited outside, ever vigilant. Walking into the small, two-story home, two women went upstairs looking at the floor as they walked past us. In what appeared to be the family room, two other men sat. One was Jasem's father, Zafir. The other was his grandfather, Samuel, who stared at me as if he knew me, even though we had never met.

We discussed their observations. Two kilometers from their home was a small farm complex. It was there Jasem and his family believed the HVT visited every so often with a small band of 'holy warriors,' or whatever. Based on the debriefing of this family, which lasted a couple of hours into the early morning, we were convinced it was indeed the HVT they had seen going into the complex in a small white car. But most surprising was Jasem's claim the HVT was there now.

"Where?" I asked, not really understanding Jasem, who spoke near perfect English.

"There. At the complex. If you drive near it you will see two cars parked outside of the main gate, each with an armed gunman either in a car or standing near it," Jasem explained.

"Let me be clear. Are you saying we're just two kilometers away from the HVT right at this moment?" I realized how stupid I sounded after I asked the question.

"Yes, yes, I thought this is why you came," Jasem said.

I just couldn't believe my good fortune! *Could it possibly be true?!* I quickly came up with a plan and, through my radio, told the scouts to leave their positions and move to the rally point south of the village where they would be picked up by us within the hour. Soon the sun would begin to rise.

Before I left, Samuel, whom I had noticed constantly staring at me as if he wanted to say something to me, finally spoke. His words were not in any language I had heard before.

"Samuel would like for you to have some Turkish coffee before you leave," Jasem told me, gesturing for me to sit next to Samuel.

"What language is that?" I asked Jasem, looking at Samuel as I moved next to sit next to him.

Jasem looked at Samuel, as if seeking permission, then Samuel smiled and nodded. "It is Aramaic, the language of Jesus Christ," said Jasem.

I stared in disbelief, I knew only a small percentage of people in the world spoke that language, and those who did were fiercely proud of their abilities. All three men in this home spoke it.

Now, at this point, time and space just seemed to disappear. It was as if this moment was the only thing that mattered in the world… it was very surreal. In a way, I almost don't even remember it all, at least not in a logical sequence. I remember sitting there with Samuel as he told me about our mutual names… SAM. I really can't recall the entire story, but he told me our name had something to do with "that of God." I remember feeling totally serene in the presence of this man.

I finished my coffee, and he had me turn the cup over on the saucer. After about five minutes, he picked up the cup and looked into it. Still speaking in Aramaic and interpreted by Jasem, he began to tell me things about myself. He said he knew I had many sons, the oldest of which was growing up too fast and beginning to act "more like a teenager." It was true, and it was much to my dissatisfaction.

He also told me I had a celebration coming up, perhaps an anniversary or more likely a birthday. He was correct; my birthday was coming up soon. I would be receiving a rather nice gift, he mentioned, but he quickly stated he didn't believe it had anything to do with my birthday.

Then he went on to tell me that I had been chosen to lead, and that is what I did. He told me I had natural leadership ability, a real ability to connect with others, that this important trait pleased God Himself, and that I should not take the responsibility lightly. I never did.

"You have been tested in life, over and over again, and your chosen profession has placed you in many moral and ethical dilemmas. Each time you have passed God's tests. But you are tormented by specific actions you have undertaken in the name of justice. One particular decision haunts you still," he said.

I simply nodded in confirmation of his statements; it was as if he was looking at my soul. I thought to myself, *how could this man possibly know so much about me? Was this some kind of spiritual witchcraft? No, this man spoke Aramaic, and was a Christian, not a Muslim. We had almost the same name.* Out here, right in the middle of the desert of the cradle of civilization, a man speaking Aramaic, Jesus' tongue, was telling me about my demons, as we prepared to kill or capture an HVT! How ironic was that!?!

"A blonde woman will free your soul from these demons with her holy words. You will once again feel like you did in your youth, and you will finally be ready for the grand plan the Lord has in store for you next," Samuel prophesied softly, almost in a whisper.

Tracy. He must be talking about my dear friend, Tracy. I could imagine no other woman enlightening me in this manner except her. She was a devout Catholic and a woman of strong faith. Tracy was married to one of my childhood friends. I looked forward to calling her when this was over to see what she had to say about all of this.

"You must leave before the morning prayer, lest you be seen," Jasem said, following his interpretation of his grandfather's words and snapping me back to reality.

"Right. ALAMO," I said into the radio, signaling my men that it was time to go. Time would later reveal to me the true identity of this blonde (spoiler alert, as it turned out it was not Tracy and in fact, I had not yet even met the woman he was referring to), but I had no idea the hell I would endure before she finally found me. And therein lies the story of my incredible journey of how this counterspy ended up an obedient disciple of Jesus.

PART ONE
IN THE BEGINNING

1
THE ARNET BENSON

 "The Lord tests the righteous, but his soul hates the wicked and the one who loves violence." – Psalm 11:5

GROWING UP IN THE MEXICAN-AMERICAN-DOMINATED, Arnet Benson barrio of Lubbock, Texas, was akin to living by prison rules, without actually being locked up. You kept to yourself, always minding your own business. You never talked to cops, and you always turned a blind eye to the illegal activities of the neighbors. This is a place where snitches really do get stitches. If you were affiliated, meaning you ran with a gang, then you naturally had instant enemies in rival gangs. Even if you didn't run with a gang, if you hung out with a group of friends, then many times gangs would just assume you and your friends were a gang, and that meant trouble. Drugs were readily available everywhere, and all types. It was not uncommon for my family members to use drugs in plain sight, even in the front yard of my grandma's house, which was the gathering spot for all my aunts, uncles, and cousins. My grandmother's front yard had a huge tree with thick branches that provided shade for the entire front yard. As a young kid during summer barbeques, parties, or get-togethers, I would often climb up in the tree and just watch everyone go about their good time; drinking, eating, dancing, using drugs, and sometimes even fighting with each other.

I loved when my cousins would come over for parties. A few of them were my age, and we would play with cars in the backyard, or hide and seek, or just ride our bikes up and down the street. Sometimes my grandfather would give all of us a dollar and send us off to buy candy at the local neighborhood convenience store. Stinets, as it was called, was only two blocks away from my grandparents' house, and they sold all kinds of candy, ice cream, soda, chewing gum, and even had a couple of arcade games. I loved riding my bike there or just walking there with my cousins. It made us feel all grown up to have some money in our pockets. As kids, we were always mindful that trouble could be just around the corner in our neighborhood, but we weren't afraid, and it never kept us from having a good time. You just watched your surroundings as best as any kid could, and then ran as fast as any kid could if there was trouble, like a shooting, a stabbing, or a violent fight. The Arnet Benson was a violent neighborhood, not just because of gangs, but because people in this neighborhood were poor and often abused alcohol and each other.

I remember once at a backyard party at my grandma's house, one of my uncles on one side of the family got in a fight with an uncle on the other side of my family. The short story is a knife was pulled, and one of my uncles who was not even involved ended up with a huge laceration to his arm. Had my dad not placed a makeshift tourniquet on it, the doctor said my uncle may have bled to death.

In another instance of violence, my grandfather was shot in the head while stopped at a stop sign. The bullet grazed his head and he survived, but another few millimeters and he would likely have been killed. He is still alive as of the writing of this book and still lives in the Arnet Benson. He is as tough as they come. My grandfather was born and raised in Texas. He had no education but learned to make a living as a ranch hand, going from ranch to ranch helping out where he could. He met my grandmother at one such ranch and fell in love. But that's a whole other story!

One day, one of my uncles was saying hello to someone at a local park whom my uncle thought was a friend. As he gave the guy a standard bro hug, the guy had a knife in his hand and cut my uncle's right cheek, leaving him a prominent scar. My uncle pushed him away, pulled out a gun, and shot and killed him. That was when I learned that sometimes the wolf comes in sheep's clothing. I was only five years old at the time.

Most people in the Arnet Benson live well under the poverty line. Men and women work in auto service shops, bakeries, grocery stores, butcher shops, and restaurants, in construction, or as painters. They live month to month and most have no retirement plan or savings. My family was certainly no exception. One time my grandfather on my mother's side paid us an unannounced visit. My dad had been laid off from his construction job, and my mother was keeping food on the table working as an office clerk. For whatever reason, my grandfather took it upon himself to open our refrigerator, much to the surprise and discomfort of my parents. What he found totally astounded him. The fridge was empty, except for half a gallon of milk and one baked potato. My grandfather turned to my mother and asked where all our food was. She replied that that's all we had, and she was saving it for my dinner meal. When my grandfather asked what we were going to eat the next day, my dad embarrassingly answered that he would figure it out then. That day, my grandfather took us all to the grocery store and bought us a couple of bags of groceries. He couldn't afford it, so he paid with a credit card he kept for emergencies.

Even though many people in the Arnet Benson were poor, it never kept them from being able to afford alcohol. As soon as people got paid, off to the liquor store they went! My uncles were no exception. Back then, Lubbock was a dry county, meaning you had to go just outside the county line to purchase alcohol. There were several stores at "La Liña," (the line, as in the county line) as my uncles would call it, where they sold beer, wine, and liquor. One particular store called Pinkie's sold the best chopped beef sandwiches in town! Anytime my uncles invited me to ride with them to La Liña, they would always buy me a chopped beef sandwich from Pinkie's. Those rides were something out of Comedy Central! My uncles were constantly cracking jokes and telling funny stories, some of them were dirty jokes, and my uncles always warned me that if I ever told anyone about anything I heard when I was with them, I would never be allowed to hang out with them again. So I always kept my mouth shut about what I would hear when I was around them! That is when I learned to keep secrets!

Two of my uncles played in a local Tejano band and as a result were always practicing in my grandma's garage. I truly enjoyed hanging out with them; I thought they were the coolest guys on the planet because between the two of them they could play the guitar, bass, drums, saxophone, keyboard synthesizer, and the accordion. Oh, and they could also sing!

I didn't like the Tejano genre of music at first, but with so much exposure to it, I grew to really enjoy it. Tejanos are Mexican Americans, born and raised in Texas. They are proud, passionate people with a deep sense of culture and tradition. One of the best descriptions of what it's like to be a Mexican American can be found in the movie, *Selena*. In one scene, Edward James Olmos, who plays Selena's dad, is talking to her and her brother on a road trip. He tells her, "Being Mexican American is tough, Anglos jump all over you if you don't speak English perfectly, Mexicans jump all over you if you don't speak Spanish perfectly. We gotta be twice as perfect as everybody else . . . Our family has been here for centuries, and yet they treat as if we just swam across the Rio Grande. I mean, we gotta know about John Wayne AND Pedro Infante. We gotta know about Frank Sinatra AND Agustin Lara. We gotta know about Oprah AND Christina. Anglo food is too bland, and when we go to Mexico, we get the runs! Now that to me is embarrassing! Japanese Americans, Italian Americans, German Americans, their homeland is on the other side of the ocean. OURS is right next door. Right over there. And we gotta prove to the Mexicans how Mexican we are, and we gotta prove to the Americans how American we are. We gotta be MORE Mexican than the Mexicans and MORE American than the Americans, both at the same time! It's exhausting!"

Anytime my uncles had a gig in a local bar, I would go with them. I would help them offload and set up equipment. Then I would sit in the bar somewhere near the stage and drink root beer because it made me feel cool drinking something with the word "beer" in the name. My uncles would drink actual beer all night and would never mess up on stage while playing; I thought that was incredible! Every now and then I would witness a fight while at one of their gigs, sometimes between women. My uncles would usually just keep on playing music so long as the fight didn't interfere with them doing so. It was just how things were.

I once saw a man get stabbed by another man just a few feet away from the bar stool I was sitting on next to the stage. The man who did the stabbing cleaned the blade on his victim's shirt, then folded it and stuck it in his pocket. Then he turned around and walked out. Meanwhile the victim staggered to his feet helped along by two women, bleeding profusely from his abdomen, and just walked out. My uncles never stopped playing music throughout the ordeal.

As a little kid, I was pretty soft for the neighborhood. I mean, I did not have a mean streak, I liked being clean, I trusted people easily, and I cried pretty much anytime I fell off my bike or skateboard. After my mom or dad would tell me everything was going to be ok and placed a Band-Aid on any small cuts I may have sustained, or kissed any bruises I may have gotten, I would stop crying and go play again. When a kid pushed me off my skateboard and I ran home crying, my uncles decided it was time they taught me how to fight. They would hold up their hand and tell me to punch it as hard as I could, so I would. Then they would say for me to hit it harder, and that they barely felt anything. So I would make the tightest fist I could and swing it at them as hard as possible until they would say those three validating words, "Alright, good job!"

Violence was simply something you learned to live with in the Arnet Benson. Domestic abuse was incredibly common, even within my own family. Often times I would see a female relative with a black eye or a busted lip. Sometimes I would hear stories about how one of my male relatives beat up his wife because she was talking to another man at a store or gas station. For the most part, the wife was probably just saying hello to a co-worker or childhood friend, but machismo ran wild in my family, and spouses learned quickly how to avoid angering their husbands.

I remember once when I was a kid I was at a relative's house while my parents worked. My male relative was arguing with his spouse about money. She must have grown tired of the argument, so she told me to get my shoes on because we were leaving. She began walking toward the bedroom when my male relative grabbed her by the hair and yanked her back into the living room, telling her she was not going anywhere and not to walk away from him when he was talking to her. She began to scream for him to let her go. I got scared and ran and hid in a closet while he smacked her around, then left the house. I found her laying on the couch with a busted lip and a bloody nose, crying. I grew to hate seeing a woman cry, and even more so to see one get beat up. If it happened in front of me, I felt helpless because I was just a little boy. I couldn't stop it from happening. It was during this time I vowed never to hit my wife if I was ever married.

Divorce was also very common. Every first uncle I have who has ever been married, on both my mother and my dad's side of the family, has been divorced at least once. Some more than once. Many of my cousins grew up without their biological father in their life as a result. Not all of them, but a few. And a couple of those divorces were really ugly. One of my uncles basically went to war with his ex-wife's family. I mean, they would literally conduct drive-by shootings at my uncle's house, and he would reciprocate.

If my uncle saw any of them while out in public, there was sure to be a fight.

In the Arnet Benson, one had to learn not to show weakness. You had to learn to be tough, to be aggressive. To stand up for yourself and not let others push you around, lest you pay dearly for not doing so. Some people learned to stand up for themselves, and then again, others did not. My mother would always say to me not to let other kids push me around or bully me. She was concerned about this because I was such a mama's boy! She felt my kind nature would be taken advantage of by other kids . . . or grownups.

I remember once when I was in first grade I came home from school with wet pants. My mother asked me if I had peed myself and I embarrassingly said yes. She asked me why, and I explained I had asked my teacher if I could go to the bathroom, and she had told me no. I believe she told me to wait as school was almost out. Whatever the case, my mom got extremely angry and grabbed me by the hand and marched me right back to school, cussing the whole time about how she was going to talk to my "stupid teacher." As she walked angrily into the classroom, me in tow, my teacher looked up from her desk.

"Hi," she said, smiling.

"Did you tell my son he couldn't go to the bathroom today?!" My mom said rather loudly.

"Uh, I asked him to hold it . . ."

My mom interrupted her before the teacher could go on. "You don't ever tell my son he can't go to the bathroom, do you understand me?!" my mom said, now yelling at my teacher. "Look at him! He peed his pants! And he was embarrassed! You embarrassed my son! If he ever comes home wet again, I am going to come back here and next time I won't be so nice! Do you hear me?!" As my teacher went to respond, my mom turned me around and said, "Let's go, mijo." And we left. From then on it was not uncommon for my teacher to ask me several times throughout the day if I needed to use the bathroom.

For as much struggle, pain, and suffering that occurred in the Arnet Benson, the Catholic faith ran strong through the neighborhood. My parents and I were in church most, but not every, Sunday. I found it so boring, and then having to stand up and sit down over and over again throughout the service was annoying to me. I never really complained because I was afraid if I did, my parents would make me go to the kid's area. Not sure why I didn't like going back there with the other kids, but I guess I just didn't want to leave my parents' side.

I also attended service at a Pentecostal church on the east side of town where my grandparents on my mother's side lived. My grandmother there was very faithful and never missed a Sunday service. Sometimes she'd go on Saturday as well and drag all of us grandkids with her. There were three of us grandkids who would go, myself and my two cousins, Rheanna and Delila. Along with us would also be my Uncle Joey, who was only a couple of years older than me and the youngest of my grandmother's nine kids. My two cousins would sing and play their tambourines while my grandmother would get on her knees and worship, often crying and screaming out to Jesus. It was somewhat scary for me and nothing like the Catholic church I normally attended with my parents and my other grandparents. Both my Uncle Joey and I were always happy when it was time to go home from church services. But it was these two churches that laid the foundation for my faith as I grew older and eventually moved away. Even though my mother was raised Pentecostal her whole life, when she married my dad, she changed over to Catholicism like my dad and his family. They also decided they would raise their kids Catholic as well. So when we finally did move away, we continued practicing in the Catholic faith. A faith that never really stuck to me despite completing all of my sacraments. Most confusing was watching family members and family friends proclaim their love of Jesus on Sundays at church, then live a life completely opposite of the Catholic faith Monday through Saturday (I realize there are people like this in all denominations, not just Catholicism). This was the example that was set before me as a child.

2

CHANGING THE TRAJECTORY

> *"For I know the plans I have for you, declares the Lord, plans for welfare and not for evil, to give you a future and a hope." –Jeremiah 29:11*

MY MOM and dad met while attending Lubbock High School. She was from another barrio on the east side of town. At first she wanted nothing to do with my dad, as she found him cocky and immature. The fact he is two years younger than her might have had something to do with that. He would ask my mom out on a date, and she would tell him to go away. My mother grew up with eight other siblings, five brothers and three sisters. She was the oldest sister, and the second child born to my grandmother. My mom learned early on how to sacrifice for the family. She had no social life, as her days were filled with school then coming home to help my grandmother care for her younger siblings. She would cook, clean, sew, wash clothes in a washtub, wash dishes, and every now and then if there was time, she would play in the backyard with her younger siblings. But that was rare.

On the weekends there was more cleaning to be done, as well as church. Everyone but my grandfather had to go to church. My grandfather didn't believe in God, and at times he would get angry with how much time my grandmother devoted to Jesus. My grandmother would make her kids take time to pray and would often have them singing worship songs in Spanish in the living room. Every day, my grandmother would go into her small, walk-in closet, shut the door, get on her knees, and pray for twenty or thirty minutes. As a young child, I could hear my grandmother praying in the closet of her bedroom. I couldn't always make out the words, but I could hear her mumbling something, and then she would start crying. It sounded to me as if she were in physical pain as she cried and prayed out loud. I would get scared and run to my mom, who would smile and explain to me my grandmother wasn't in pain or even sad, that she was just happy to be in the presence of God. I did not understand that at all. How could I? I was just a little kid! So I would avoid going near my grandmother's bedroom door whenever I knew she was in her closet praying to God.

My mom was not allowed to date or have boyfriends. So when my dad was trying to court her, she knew it was not possible because her parents would not allow it. I think that was probably the real reason she did not give my dad the time of day. But my dad was persistent and eventually, behind the backs of her parents, my mom agreed to date my dad. She would sneak out of the house and my dad would pick her up down the street. Sometimes her sisters would cover for her. She very quickly fell head over heels for my dad. Then one day, when my dad was just sixteen years old and my mother was eighteen, they eloped. One of my dad's friends, Pete Albiar, agreed to be their witness and so they tied the knot. When my dad brought my mom to his home that day and explained to his parents how they were now married, my grandmother was horrified!

"Take her back!" my grandmother yelled at my dad in Spanish.

"Mom, how can I take her back? She is my wife now!" my dad replied.

My grandmother cringed at the word wife. "You take her back right now, Bobby!"

He explained, "Mom, we're married now by law. I can't do that."

"Oh my God, I can't believe this is happening. I can't believe you did this!" she yelled.

The reaction on my mom's side was much more restrained.

"Well, I guess you need to go with Bobby now, Gina. You're his wife now," my grandfather said to his daughter, my mom.

"Thank you, dad!" my mom said to him, crying her eyes out.

My grandfather turned to my dad and said, "You better take care of her. Treat her right."

"I will, father-in-law," my dad said before departing with my mom.

They eventually both dropped out of high school and joined the work force, renting their own place in the Arnet Benson, where my mom became pregnant with me.

My dad and I have always had a good relationship, and it remains tight to this day. As a child, he never beat or verbally abused me. He was a very loving father. My mother was the same. She kept me clean and well-dressed and never laid a hand on me in anger. She and I have always had a tight relationship as well. I am convinced that if I was ever to commit a murder, my mom would help me bury the body to avoid me having to go to jail!

    I was a well-behaved kid, according to my parents. I never had temper tantrums or acted up in front of company or anything like that. But I was a momma's boy. I didn't like to be left with anyone who wasn't family. So when my mom tried to leave me at a day care facility, I ended up crying and crying until the staff eventually had to call my mom and tell her to come get me. As a result, I would often be left with my grandma on my dad's side, who worked cleaning rooms at a local motel, but her shift didn't end until later in the day. I would actually be left alone in the house for hours. My grandmother would make me some eggs and toast, or chorizo and eggs, and leave it on the table for me covered by a paper towel. I would grab a juice bottle from the refrigerator then sit down to eat my breakfast. Then I would watch morning cartoons in the living room until my Uncle Robert would come home during his lunch hour to pick me up. I loved this because Uncle Robert drove a motorcycle, and I would ride on the back, clutched to my uncle for dear life as he would speed off to take me somewhere to eat, usually a hamburger at a local spot. Then he would return me to my grandmother's house while he sat and watched cartoons with me for just a few minutes before he had to go back to work. An hour or so later, my mom or my grandmother (depended on their work shift) would return from work. It would be years later when I would learn how important it is for boys to have good male role models around, whether it is their own dad (preferable) or a close family friend or relative. The fact my uncle spent just about an hour each day with me, talking to me and watching cartoons with me,

I believe was of great benefit for me. I felt loved, wanted, and seen. Sometimes that's all kids need.

One of my dad's best friends, Pete Albiar, had enlisted in the Army when I was still pretty young. When he was home on leave, he would sit with my dad and regale him with stories of the training he received, the places he'd visited, and all the benefits and pay he received as a result of signing up. He planted seeds in my dad's head about military service. But my dad wasn't sure he was cut out for all of the physical activity and early mornings that come with the Army lifestyle. It was a very disciplined way of living compared to life in the Arnet Benson.

My brother was soon born, and as my dad looked around, what he saw bothered him. Men struggling to provide for their families, resorting to dealing drugs or a life of crime just to make ends meet. Children growing up and falling into the same cycle and witnessing violent crimes first-hand by the age of five years old. He noticed many of his friends and family members were in and out of jail. A very small percentage of friends went on to college, and some to the military. But so many of them were stuck in a perpetual cycle of survival. My dad asked himself if this was the kind of life he wanted my brother and me to have. He wondered if he could break the cycle for his family. It played out in his mind for a long time until one day, he woke up and decided he was going to do it. He was going to enlist in the Army.

And he did just that. Within two days of making up his mind, he was gone. I remember crying every time I realized he was gone. At night, in the morning, after school. I was the biggest cry baby ever! My mom, brother, and I moved in with my grandparents on my dad's side, right there in the Arnet Benson. And whenever my dad would call us from Fort Sill, Oklahoma, where he was attending Basic Training, I would cry just hearing his voice. It got so bad that every time he called, my mother would tell me not to cry or she would not let me speak to him. As a kid there was no way for me to know just how much my crying impacted my dad. I am sure he did not want to hear me cry out of sadness, it probably broke his heart each time, causing him to second guess his decision to enlist. But he kept his eye on the fact he was making a better future for his family by serving our country.

Eventually he graduated all of his training and we were stationed at Fort Carson, Colorado. But after a year, he came down on orders for Korea. It was a one-year, unaccompanied tour. Meaning he had to go alone, without his family, without us! Once again, I was heartbroken, and I grew to hate the Army. I hated his decision to join because it meant he kept leaving us. We went back to Lubbock to live with my grandparents in the Arnet Benson, where for the next year, I witnessed more violence, more men abusing their spouses, more drug deals, and more divorces. It never dawned on me that my dad's decision to join the Army meant I would soon leave the Arnet Benson forever. I mean, we'd come back and visit, but I would not have to grow up there. He had broken the cycle I was destined for in that neighborhood, he had changed the trajectory of our lives forever, and for the better. As a kid, I just did not understand that. I had no idea how the opportunities found in better schools, better neighborhoods, and just overall better environments would help me develop more as a kid and into adulthood. But I would eventually get it.

After my dad returned from Korea, the Army took us to live at Fort Polk, Louisiana. We lived on the base in a nice, brand-new housing division. Everything about this neighborhood was nice, including the neighbors! It was a far cry from the Arnet Benson.

And when my grandparents came to visit, they kept telling us we were rich! Something no one else in the history of the world ever said to someone living on Fort Polk! We were not rich of course, but our quality of life was such that anyone who came to visit us from the Arnet Benson immediately thought we were! It was here that I developed more as a kid, with opportunities simply not possible for me back in Lubbock. I played in a little league flag-football team, then t-ball, and I also joined the Cub Scouts. I remember once my dad helped me carve out a very cool-looking derby car from a block of wood to race in the Cub Scouts tournament. It didn't win, but it was the coolest looking car there!

My friends and I would explore the woods behind our house, where it was rumored some kind of beast lived. Of course, there was no such thing, but it was fun pretending there was and scaring other younger kids with stories of how the creature ate little kids. My friends and I would ride our bikes everywhere, then hang out playing football until the streetlights came on. Once, we even built a tree house near the tree line of the woods behind our house. We would bring food and drinks to consume inside of it while we sat and told each other lies, and then one day one of my friends brought a Playboy magazine to the tree house. I had never seen a naked woman before, and we all pointed and giggled at the ladies. I was only ten years old.

All of that fun and debauchery ended when my dad received orders for Europe. We were heading off to Baumholder, Germany, for the next three years. I was crushed. For some reason, I had this huge hang up about celebrating my thirteenth birthday in Germany.

"I don't want to be a German teenager!" I remember telling my parents. They really didn't know what to say to that. It was so incredibly ridiculous, but for some reason it was a big deal to me. I am not sure why I felt becoming a teenager had to be done in the U.S., but that's how I felt at the time, and it caused me much grief as there was no way to avoid the inevitable. So, off to Europe we went.

Germany turned out to be a great time. I made some great friends, kissed a girl for the first time, learned to ski, and got to see some awesome castles along the Rhein-River. School field trips included activities like visiting the city of Trier, seeing a live performance of The Nutcracker, skiing in Austria, and going to Idar Oberstein to see a church that was built into the side of a cliff with one side of it exposed. I mean, half of the church was literally stuck into the side of the cliff, with only the steeple side on the outside. Legend had it that two brothers who once lived in the castle at the top of the cliff fell in love with the same woman. They had a fight, and one brother pushed the other over the cliff. He was so saddened and grief stricken that he built the church into the side of the cliff as a memorial to his dead brother.

And yes, I finally turned thirteen years of age before we left there. I was a German teenager! My parents threw me a big surprise birthday party at the local Youth Center on base. One of the girls I was madly smitten with was there and she kissed me that night, making me feel invincible! All of a sudden, my hang up about becoming a German teenager disappeared.

Following an amazing three-year tour in Germany, we moved to Fort Campbell, Kentucky, home of the 101st Airborne Division (Air Assault). My dad was proud to be serving in one of the most famous, fiercest fighting units in the U.S. Army's arsenal. Fort Campbell sits on the border of Kentucky and Tennessee; the state line literally runs right through the middle of the base. But the main post office resides on the Kentucky side, making it the official location for the base.

I made some really good friends there. That was also the place where my heart was first broken by a girl. Yep, she ripped it out and stomped on it! I learned a hard lesson in love . . . mainly that sometimes nice guys finish last. She left me for a pot-smoking, leather jacket wearing, mustang driving, heavy metal listening, long-haired sixteen-year-old (two years older than both her and I). I didn't smoke anything, wore a windbreaker, wasn't old enough to drive yet, listened to rock but not heavy metal, and wore my hair short! I wondered why she had ever dated me to begin with. But for the next year I saw her pull up to school in his mustang and then walk into school holding his hand. It was hard to watch. But what I later learned made all of that seem like child's play. Rumor had it, he took her virginity. I am pretty sure my heart stopped beating the moment when I learned that. I moved on with my broken heart.

Over thirty-five years later, I am still friends and in touch with some of the people I went to school with at Fort Campbell. While I was living there, the Space Shuttle Challenger exploded in mid-air shortly after takeoff. We watched the re-runs in science class following the breaking news. In honor of the teacher who was one of the crew members, we did not do anything else at school that day except talk about the incident and watch the news in class. Another teacher brought her kids into our classroom to watch the news. I guess they did not have a TV in their classroom. My friends and I sat together and talked softly about the incident. It was a sad day across America.

It was while being stationed at Fort Campbell that my father was selected to be an Army Recruiter. Being a recruiter meant we could literally end up living anywhere in the country, regardless of whether or not there was a military base around. While my dad was attending recruiter training and approaching his graduation date, he called home to tell us where the Army was sending him to recruit our nation's future soldiers . . . Los Angeles, California.

3
URBAN JUNGLE

> *"No temptation has overtaken you that is not common to man. God is faithful, and he will not let you be tempted beyond your ability, but with the temptation he will also provide the way of escape, that you may be able to endure it." – 1 Corinthians 10:13*

NOBODY in my family had ever been to Los Angeles before. Driving in on Interstate 10 from Arizona, it took us literally hours to cross LA to get to Simi Valley, where we would live through my junior high and high school years. I had never been to a place where you could drive for hours and never see a country road! This place was an urban jungle, and a far cry from any place we had ever lived. Little did I know how much this place would challenge my family and me.

Walking onto the campus at Valley View Junior High School, I found it strange there were no enclosed hallways. All classrooms opened up to an outside walkway. There was a huge quad in the center of the campus where most students hung out during lunch. Wall lockers were situated along the outdoor walkways. This was a totally different school than the Department of Defense, or DoD, schools I had attended since the second grade. I found out just how different when I walked into a bathroom. The mirrors were boarded up, and the entire inside was spray painted with graffiti. Some kid was taking a smoke break in the corner while another kid sat on one of the sinks while he chatted with the smoker. Both of them looked like skaters, from their hairstyle to their worn-out Vans, and seemed like they could hold their own in the half pipe.

My dad worked late hours in those days. Recruiters back then were under a lot of pressure to get high school graduates into the Army, and my dad was good at it. He enjoyed the fact he could offer young kids from the various low-income neighborhoods in LA an opportunity to make a guaranteed paycheck every month with full medical and dental benefits, a place to live at no cost to them, and three square meals a day, free at first, then extremely affordable afterwards. Not to mention the chance to learn a trade while getting paid for learning it, and opportunities for travel around the world! I witnessed many kids, especially Mexican American kids, take my dad up on the opportunity to serve their country with full pay and benefits. I remember so many parents of those kids would thank my dad profusely for recruiting their sons, many of whom were headed for a life of gang violence, drugs, and crime had my dad not found them and convinced them to join the Army.

"You think you're tough?" he would say to any one of them. "Well, the Army will make you tougher. They'll show you how to fight. They'll show you how to shoot different types of pistols, rifles, and machine guns. You can drive a tank if you want or learn to fire a cannon. Or you can become a medic and learn how to save lives. You can even go airborne and jump out of planes! They will also get you into the best physical shape of your life! Oh, and I haven't even told you about the free health care and all of the other benefits!" My dad could relate to them given his background and upbringing in the Arnet Benson neighborhood of Lubbock, Texas.

As I grew older, I started hanging out with the wrong crowd. Don't get me wrong, they were all good kids mostly, but we were all a bunch of wannabe gang bangers. I was always out to prove I was a tough guy and got into many fights in high school. I won most, but not all! After I got my driver's license, it was game on. My dad helped me buy an old '69 Chevy Impala, and away I went. I would go explore the greater Los Angeles area with my friends, I mean, we would drive everywhere. Some of my friends had family in the city, so we would go visit them up to two hours away. I got to know the urban jungle like the back of my hand. Pretty soon, I also knew where the drugs were.

I experimented with a few hard drugs while in high school and while working part-time as a bus boy in a Mexican restaurant. The owner's son dealt cocaine from the restaurant, and eventually I began using it too. That was short-lived though, because after I caught myself craving it, I immediately gave it up out of fear I was addicted. I had seen addicts in the Arnet Benson, and I did not want to be one of them, so I quit before I got truly addicted. It didn't stop me from experimenting with other drugs though, but I never became a regular user of anything. Except maybe alcohol.

Every Friday my friends and I were on a mission to find someone who could buy us some beer. Some of my friends had older brothers or sisters who would often help out in this regard. Other times we would depend on that one guy common to every town who never got a real job and just never really grew up, so he hung around high school kids as a result. You know the type. The one who could get alcohol and drugs, had been in and out of jail, still lived with his parents and sometimes would back you up in a fight. The one you thought was the coolest guy in town . . . yeah, that guy.

Beer runs were common where I grew up, and I excelled in those. It is when you walk into a gas station or some other local convenient store, peruse items inside until you get to the beer. Then you grab a twelve-pack and walk toward the cashier as if you're going to pay for it, then make a run for the door. A friend would be waiting in a car just outside the main entrance and that's how you made your getaway. I never got busted, but looking back, it was such a dumb thing to do. To be clear I am not proud of any of this, just telling it like it is/was.

A group of us once met at a Burger King parking lot in Simi Valley, waiting for our friend, Dave, to show up with one of his friends who apparently had a fake ID. As Dave pulled up and parked near us, his friend stepped out of the car wearing a miniskirt and small white boots, with the longest, most beautiful dark hair I had ever seen. Her name was Tricia, and I wanted her to be mine from the moment I saw her. She was the one with the fake ID; she was seventeen years old. All of my friends walked up and handed her some money with an order for alcohol. I wanted to talk to her, so I waited until everyone else had given her money to approach her.

"Hi," I said to her.

"Hey," she replied

"What's your name?" I asked her, a bit nervous.

She looked at me for a second before responding, "Tricia. What do you want?" She was referring to the alcohol.

"Well, my name is Sammy. Uh, can you get me a bottle of Night Train?" I said, only having had it once in my entire fifteen years of existence.

"Night Train? How old are you, Sammy?" she asked me.

"I'm fifteen," I said, a bit confused by the question.

"Fifteen?! You're just a little boy, you need to go home to your mama," she told me, giggling and smiling.

"I'll show you a little boy!" I responded, offended by her comment.

"Whatever," she said. "Hurry up and give me your money."

I gave her some cash and then met her and Dave later that night at the party that was planned at my friend Art's house. I kept staring at her all night and finally mustered up the guts to ask her for her phone number.

"How much is the bet?" she said.

I had no idea what she was referring to. "What bet?"

"The bet you made with your friends on whether or not you could get my phone number!" she said, gesturing behind me.

When I looked back, three of my friends were looking in our direction, smiling and giggling. I guess they were just enjoying me make a mockery of myself, but there was definitely no bet made. Nonetheless, I couldn't convince Tricia of it, so I had struck out that night. I told my best friend, Saul, that she was going to be my girlfriend one day. He didn't believe me, but two years later I made good on that promise!

I had made a lot of enemies in high school because I was running around trying to be a tough guy. One particular enemy of mine was a skinhead white supremacist. He hated me because I was not white, and I had once made out with his sister, Michelle. Being that he was a racist, he considered his sister "dirty" for having kissed me. That's literally what he said to her! So he had promised me that he would find me and kill me. That was how much he hated Mexican Americans . . . or any other race for that matter. So when Tricia and I started dating, we could not be anywhere alone. I needed protection, and Saul and my other friends were that protection. Tricia once asked me why we never went anywhere alone, and I told her it was for our safety. She did not break up with me, which endeared her to me even more! I was falling in serious love.

Being that I was a troublemaker, I had a police scanner in my car. Once, when my friends and I went to raid the party of my white supremacist nemesis, Tricia stayed in my car and monitored the police scanner, with instructions to start honking the horn the second she heard police were responding to the huge fight we were about to have. It was a party like any other. Someone's parents were not home and so their kids decided to throw a wild party and invite all of their neo-Nazi friends over. There were drugs and alcohol present along with a bunch of teenagers. My friends and I walked right through the front door and just started beating up every guy there. Within minutes, I heard my car horn and so my friends and I ran out of the house, jumped in our cars and took off before the cops arrived. We even saw them coming down the street with their lights on as we left the neighborhood in the opposite direction.

While I was dating Tricia, one of my ex-girlfriends became a fatal attraction. She was not happy with me having moved on from her, and she was constantly trying to cause trouble for Tricia and me. For example, one day she and two of her friends started a fight with Tricia in a parking lot, for no other reason than the fact Tricia was my girlfriend. Although Tricia held her own pretty well, I could not let them continue fighting so a couple of my friends and I broke it up. On another occasion my ex-girlfriend tossed a stuffed rabbit I had previously given her for Easter in the bed of my truck . . . on fire. So now, anytime Tricia and I went out, we had to be on the lookout for skinheads and my ex-girlfriend!

However, the icing on the cake was on one hot summer day. My little brother and I were home alone while my parents both worked. There was a knock at the door, and I got up to answer it. When I opened the front door, there, standing on the other side of the storm door were two big, Italian men in really nice suits. A tall one and a short fat one. The short one reached for the storm door and opened it before I could do or say anything. They were both scary-looking tough guys. After opening the door, the short one said to me, "Do you know (my ex-girlfriend's name which I won't divulge out of respect for her)?"

I probably should have said no, but he scared me into telling him the truth. "Yes sir." It was all I could muster.

He repeated his question even though I had already answered it. This time he brought his big fat sausage finger up to my face and said, "Do you know (ex-girlfriend)?"

"Yes sir, I do." My mind was now racing thinking about what these two had planned for me.

He leaned in close with his sausage finger still in my face as he said, "You don't know her anymore, you got me kid?"

I took a step back, looked at both of them and said, "Uh . . . yes sir, I understand."

Again, he repeated himself but this time a little louder. "You don't know her any f*#%ing more!"

"Yes sir!" I said. What else could I say? For a second there, I thought the tall one was going to pull out a pistol with a silencer and shoot me dead right there near my front door. But they just stared at me for what seemed like an eternity. Another thought entered my mind. What if they wanted me to take a "ride" with them? I had seen the movie *Goodfellas*, and enough Godfather movies and Soprano episodes to know I would not be returning from a "ride" with them and would probably end up "sleeping with the fishes!"

But as God would have it, they simply turned around and left. I never saw them again, thank God.

After dating through the summer and then through my senior year, two days after graduation, Tricia and I got married. We had a wedding service at the Sea Bee Chapel on Port Hueneme, then a reception at the local Officer's Club. My dad's active-duty status facilitated cheaper rates on the Naval Base, so we took full advantage. My dad's Army Recruiter friends even formed a Saber Squad, borrowing swords from the Marine recruiters! They just wanted to make it that much more special for us, and we appreciated the gesture. My mom and dad did everything they could to make our wedding extra special. They later told me they didn't want Tricia and me to struggle like they had. My dad kept pushing me to join the Air Force, but I wanted to be like him.

In my eyes, my dad was a great man. He had made a decision back in 1977 in Lubbock, Texas to leave the life we were then destined for and change it forever. His decision to join the United States Army ended up having an impact of monumental proportions on future generations of Villelas. I ended up obtaining a better education then I ever would have in Lubbock. I developed more as a kid playing sports and joining the Scouts, something I would have never done in Lubbock. Although I started to stray from this positive environment when we moved to LA, it wasn't enough to ruin my future.

Because of his encouragement for me to make a better life for myself in the future, I decided to join the Army. I wanted to be just like him, but he wanted a better quality of life for me, and so he kept advising me to join the Air Force. I thought about how ironic this was because my dad was an Army Recruiter at the time! But there was no way I was going to give up the manly life of a soldier for the easy and unmanly ways of the Air Force . . . just kidding Air Force dudes, you know I love y'all! I never regretted my decision to join the Army though.

But what to do as a member of the world's greatest Army, what to specialize in? This was not a simple question to answer. I wanted to do something where I could make a difference in the world. I wanted a job that came with a certain amount of adventure, even a small amount of risk. Being young, I wanted something exciting to do that would get my adrenaline flowing!

"An MP?! You don't want to stand around a gate or be a guard all the time, do you?!" my dad said.

I thought being a Military Police officer would be quite ironic given all the time I had spent avoiding the LAPD as a teenager. Thank God my dad talked me out of that one!

"How about this?" I said, pointing to a job description for Military Occupational Specialty (MOS) 97B, Special Agent, Counterintelligence. It was in some Army regulation with all the MOS codes for the various jobs I was qualified for (somehow I'd managed to score pretty high on the test!).

"Yeah, I'm not sure what they do, but sometimes they wear civilian clothes and investigate people's backgrounds and stuff," My dad explained, piquing my curiosity.

"That's the one I want! I want to check people out and stuff, investigate bad guys, all of that sounds pretty neat," I said, not really understanding what I was getting myself into.

Before leaving for Basic Training, some newspaper reporter from the local paper in Simi Valley interviewed my dad and me and then ran a story titled, "FATHER RECRUITS SON FOR COUNTERSPY WORK." One of my teachers saw the article and thought it was very interesting and embarrassed me by pinning up the article in her classroom. My dad cut the article out of the paper; I still have it to this day.

4

A SOLDIER

> *"And I heard the voice of the Lord saying, "Whom shall I send, and who will go for us?" Then I said, "Here I am! Send me.""* – Isaiah 6:8

SHORTLY AFTER ARRIVING to Basic Training at Fort Jackson, South Carolina, the summer of 1990, just one month after graduating high school and then marrying my high school sweetheart, my dad sent me a poem that I desperately needed to hear. It arrived at a time when I doubted whether or not I had made the right decision to sign up to be a soldier. I was beginning to doubt whether or not I could handle the rigid lifestyle, the early mornings, and the lack of sleep! The poem was titled simply, "A SOLDIER." It went like this:

I was that which others did not want to be.

I went where others feared to go, and did what others failed to do.

I asked nothing from those who gave nothing, and reluctantly accepted the thought of eternal loneliness, should I fail.

I have seen the face of terror, felt the stinging cold of fear, and enjoyed the sweet taste of a moment's love.

I have cried, pained, and hoped. But most of all, I have lived times others would say were best forgotten.

At least someday I will be able to say that I was proud of what I was ... A SOLDIER.

The author remains unknown. This poem gave me new life and motivation . . . I was now determined to earn the title of SOLDIER.

For the next several weeks, I took in everything the Drill Sergeants were teaching us. Everything from rifle marksmanship, to field operations, to physical fitness. One thing Drill Sergeants know how to do is get you out of your civilian mindset and make you start thinking like a soldier. Their job is to strip away all of that selfish thinking that cannot be tolerated on the battlefield. Before you know it, you are sharing your canteen with your buddy without thinking, you are completing your cleaning tasks in the barracks, and then asking who else needs help. You begin working as a team the more you spend time together eating, training, struggling, overcoming challenges, and winning. You form a tightknit bond with each other. When it came time for graduation, those of us who made it could hardly believe that day had come when the Drill Sergeants no longer yelled at us. They now addressed us by our rank and last name. We had earned it. We had earned the right to be called a soldier.

This is how it starts. This is how the U.S. Army begins training and developing its future leaders. The Department of Defense is the number one leadership institution in the world. No other organization produces leaders of such high quality because war demands it. If you can lead men and women in combat, you can lead them anywhere. Just think about how many books have been written on the topic of leadership specifically for the civilian population by strong military leaders. Several Navy SEALS, Army Green Berets, Air Force pilots, and Marine Recon specialists have all found a way to take leadership concepts, principles and experiences and superimpose them onto civilian jobs. Everyone from high-level CEOs and corporate executives to blue-collar workers and housewives can learn a thing or two, or three, from the military's finest. Why do you think civilians love hiring veterans? Because of the work ethic, the discipline, the dependability, and numerous other characteristics found in veterans and gained from a lifetime of service to our country in the world's finest military.

When you are battling PTSD, perhaps you have forgotten just how valuable your skillset is for having served in the military. Think about all of the annual, mandatory training you received while in the military. Sexual Harassment/Assault Response and Prevention training, Equal Employment Opportunity training, Ethics training, Constitution Day training, Information Security training, Cyber Awareness training, Risk Management training, Employee Safety training, Trafficking in Persons training . . . civilian employers love this! And you should always highlight this training on a resume for civilian employers to see.

If you are a civilian employer, are these not excellent courses to have been trained in? Military veterans undergo much more training than just combat training, or specific job training;

therefore, they can be counted on to not just get the job done, but get it done right! The veteran population is a vast pool of skills that stem beyond the obvious. But not all civilians understand that, making it frustrating for separating servicemen and women who are transitioning to the civilian job market. But I digress.

Upon graduating from Basic Combat Training, I arrived at Riley Barracks on Fort Huachuca, Arizona. The airport shuttle pulled up to the front of the main entrance to a three-story cinder block building that was to be my home for the next six months. It was a cool, clear, and sunny day. I stepped out of the shuttle to see a slew of activity. There were people standing around in shorts, t-shirts, and shower shoes just talking, others were carrying duffle bags out of the barracks, and a few were being yelled at by two Drill Sergeants, who had them doing pushups on the cement slab in front of the building. They were all young, mostly my age group. Groups of guys and girls were walking with each other, or just standing around talking with one another. Cars would pull up with more people, and some cars departed the parking lot with other people. It was like arriving on a college campus, except with mean Drill Sergeants!

I was here to be trained and certified as a Counterintelligence Special Agent, or as the Drill Sergeants referred to me, a "CI guy." A CI guy is basically a counterspy, or spy catcher. CI guys have to be better than the spies they aim to detect, identify, neutralize, and/or exploit. So they are trained in all manners of tradecraft, the operational security skills required to ensure secrecy of the operation and facilitate success. CI Agents often do not wear military uniforms or adhere to strict military grooming standards. To be a CI Agent, one must successfully obtain and maintain a Top-Secret security clearance and have a high enough aptitude for the complex problem solving and quick thinking required for the job. The basic mission of an Army CI Agent is to hunt down spies and terrorists. But the one thing my Drill Sergeant kept reminding me of while in training to be a CI guy, was that I was a soldier first. And a soldier's job is to blow things up and kill the enemy, period.

So while our CI instructors taught us all about espionage and terrorism in a classroom setting, our Drill Sergeants would expound on the combat tactics we learned in Basic Combat Training, and teach us new ones as well. Things such as patrolling, ambushes, hand-to-hand combat, and proper use of camouflage, cover, and concealment. Problem solving was tested and taught via what was known as the Leadership Reaction Course. It called for solving problems such as building a bridge, getting over a wall, or underneath an obstacle, with only a very limited supply of items. We had to learn to improvise, overcome, and adapt. Every challenge was timed, and the Drill Sergeants would designate a different person to be in charge of each separate challenge, who was evaluated on his/her leadership skills and ability to successfully accomplish the mission.

For example, one challenge called for us to devise a way to cross from one small, elevated platform to another at a lower elevation, without falling and using only two two-by-fours, some rope, and a tire. Everyone and every item provided had to get across as well. So we tied the two boards together at the ends, making them long enough to reach from platform A to platform B. It wasn't very sturdy, so we sent the lightest of us across first. That person then stood on the end of the board as it rested on platform B, making it a bit stronger for the next person to cross. Eventually two or three people could stand on that board over on platform B while someone crossed the makeshift bridge while carrying the tire from platform

A, (two others also stood on the board at platform A). The lighter of those two would cross last. We would then pull the two boards tied together to platform B and thereby accounting for all of the items on the other side. The Drill Sergeants truly enjoyed watching us struggle with some of the challenges. Some teams would fail, and the Drill Sergeants would descend on them like vultures on roadkill.

It was also the Drill Sergeants' job to improve our physical fitness levels. So we did a lot of running before dawn. I enjoyed the formation runs where we sang cadence. Nothing motivated me more than to sing some inspiring cadence during a morning run. My Drill Sergeant was the best at singing cadence. His name was Drill Sergeant Davis, and he sang with so much passion it would motivate us to repeat his cadence even louder. He had a real talent for taking any old song and singing it as cadence for our runs. Take the song, "I Heard it Through the Grapevine," by Marvin Gaye. Drill Sergeant Davis could sing that in perfect cadence, and he had one heck of a singing voice as well!

We also did a lot, and I mean a lot of ruck marching. Drill Sergeant Davis would take us up and down the hills on Fort Huachuca wearing full uniform and boots and carrying a thirty-pound ruck and a rifle . . . oh, and wearing our helmets! This wasn't a stroll through the country, it was fast paced. Drill Sergeant Davis would say to us, "You must be able to walk quickly through enemy territory in order to link up with the helicopter that will facilitate your extraction! The chopper cannot wait for your lazy asses to get to it! If you're not there, it will leave, and you will die at the hands of the enemy! So let's go, we gotta make it to the chopper!" And he would take off in a dead sprint! If you have never had to run in combat boots on pavement, wearing almost fifty or sixty pounds of clothing and equipment, consider yourself blessed! This is where your mind can be your most powerful weapon and can easily turn against you if you let it, as I would later learn.

A quick word on mindset. In one of the stories from the Bible, God appeared to Moses in the burning bush and told him to go to Egypt to lead the Israelites out of slavery. In response, "And Moses said, "I will turn aside to see this great sight, why the bush is not burned." Then Moses said to God, "If I come to the people of Israel and say to them, 'The God of your fathers has sent me to you,' and they ask me, 'What is his name?' what shall I say to them?" God said to Moses, "I am who I am ." And he said, "Say this to the people of Israel: 'I am has sent me to you.'"" – Exodus 3:13-14

So God is in fact the only One who can declare Himself as "I AM." For you and me, "I AM" is a false claim to our own sovereignty, because unlike God, we are not omnipresent or omniscient. As a matter of mindset, I AM are the two most powerful words in any language, for what you place after them can actually determine your reality. Words mean things, and they are very powerful! When used in acknowledgment of the fact, it is only through God's will you are made as such, and only for God's purpose, I AM can change your life! Because when used in affirmations, I AM can keep your spirit balanced, your mind focused, and your heart continuously transforming!

Here are thirteen affirmations you can recite daily, along with the bible verse they are derived from:

1. I AM a child of God. – 1 John 3:1

2. I AM prosperous and God delights in my prosperity. – Psalms 35:27
3. I AM blessed to be a blessing. – Genesis 12:2
4. I AM a lender and not a borrower. – Deuteronomy 15:6
5. I AM a person of excellence and integrity. – 1 Thessalonians 4:7
6. I AM a person who forgives easily and loves all people. – Ephesians 4:32
7. I AM the head and not the tail. – Deuteronomy 28:13
8. I AM blessed with every spiritual blessing. – Ephesians 1:3
9. I AM strong in the Lord. – Ephesians 6:10
10. I AM bold for Christ. – Acts 4:31
11. I AM a soul winner. – Matthew 4:19
12. I AM faithful and steadfast in the Lord. – 1 Corinthians 15:58
13. I AM strong in character and ready for anything. – 1 Corinthians 15:13

Back to training. Some of my fellow candidate CI guys would tell themselves they couldn't go any further and would stop running. As they fell further and further behind, Drill Sergeant Davis, leading the pack, would turn us all around to go back and pick up the stragglers.

"You're screwing your buddies!" he would yell at those who had quit running. He was right, because those of us who refused to quit would end up running longer distances because we kept having to turn around to pick up the stragglers. Pretty soon all of us were yelling to one another, "Let's go, we gotta make it to the chopper!" By the end of the cycle, nobody would quit, everyone would keep going no matter how difficult.

Drill Sergeant Davis was also an avid kick boxer and martial artists. He could fight! And he loved to fight. He drove a Harley Davidson with a biker club made up of veterans. His nickname was "Stick," not sure why though. But one day he brought us all into the gym in our PT (Physical Training) clothes. We thought we were going to work out, but instead he began teaching us fighting techniques, or hand-to-hand combat. At one point, he picked my roommates Rodriguez (a.k.a. "Rico"), Torres, Figueroa, and myself for a demonstration. He called us the "Latino Connection" because of our last names and ethnicity. He placed Rico about five feet in front of him, Figueroa behind him, and to his left he placed Torres, and me to his right flank. Then he said, "Come at me."

All four of us looked at each other in disbelief, not really understanding what it was he wanted us to do.

"What do you mean, Drill Sergeant?" I asked.

He looked at me and very calmly said, "Come at me. I want you to take me down."

"You want us to fight you?" asked Rico.

"Yes, for the love of God, yes! Now attack me!" He was yelling now.

I was standing to his right flank. I saw Figueroa begin to crouch while putting his hands up. Torres also put his hands up and began to bounce just a little bit, like a boxer. Rico was still standing there in front of Davis trying to determine if he was being serious or not. I thought to myself, *how many opportunities do you get to beat up a Drill Sergeant? I am going for it.*

I quickly began to close the distance with him, swinging my right arm around with the intention of punching him in the face.

That was the last thing I remember, because he caught me with a side-kick right in the gut, and I doubled over in pain. By the time I realized what had happened, I looked over to see Figueroa fly through the air and land on his right side. Then Davis flipped Rico over his back as he came in with a right hook; Rico hit the mat hard, knocking the wind out of him. Torres probably thought he had an advantage now that Davis had his back toward him, so he went to kick him in the back. But Davis somehow sensed Torres' approach and crouched low while spinning around with his leg outstretched, catching Torres in the shin, and knocking him to the ground. Davis jumped on top of him as if he were going to clobber him with his right fist, but suddenly he stopped. He looked around at the rest of the students who were watching with amazement, and he stood up and just smiled at the four bodies lying on the floor in pain. He walked away leaving us there on the mat. One of the other students commented that the whole scene looked like a crime scene. Everyone laughed and then helped us to our feet. Davis had whipped our butts! This scenario repeated itself until one day when we finally took him down on the mat. That day, Drill Sergeant Davis became proud of us, and that's what we wanted, his validation.

Graduating from the CI course, I was technically and tactically ready for the field. Before I left Fort Huachuca, one of my other Drill Sergeants told me, "Remember this: Bad habits last a lifetime. Good habits last only as long as there are professional, physically fit, Non-Commissioned Officers there to enforce them." Something I never forgot.

Another thing I never forgot was Drill Sergeant Davis telling me his goal was to make us intelligent barbarians, and that we should never forget we are soldiers first. Even on the days when we found ourselves wearing civilian clothes, he wanted us to remember we volunteered for the profession of arms. At the time I did not understand why he was telling us that, but I would come to understand it later on.

For the next several years, the Army would send me to all corners of the globe chasing spies and terrorists. As time went on, my experiences caused me to rethink everything I knew about being human.

PART TWO
SLIPPING INTO DARKNESS

5
THE SHEEP DOG

> *"He said to him a second time, "Simon, son of John, do you love me?" He said to him, "Yes, Lord; you know that I love you." He said to him, "Tend my sheep." –*
> ***John 21:16***

ACCORDING to U.S. Army LTC Dave Grossman, there are three kinds of people in this world. In his book, *On Combat, The Psychology and Physiology of Deadly Combat in War and Peace*, Grossman writes about the Sheep, Wolves, and Sheep Dogs. The Sheep are the common, hard-working citizens who merely want a better life for themselves and their children and are not afraid to work hard to get it. They generally live within the norms of society and do their best to abide by the law. They go about their lives doing what makes America so great. They are CEOs, farmers, truckers, pilots, hair-dressers, teachers, bankers, businessmen, entrepreneurs, plumbers, electricians, mechanics, secretaries, gas station attendants, cashiers, restaurant owners, waiters, waitresses, and so on and so forth. They are unequivocally the heart and soul of America.

Then there are Wolves. Wolves are those who can't seem to play by society's rules, who live outside of its norms and get what they want by taking it. Wolves are those who try and eat the Sheep. They rob, cheat, steal, kill, rape, pillage, and plunder. They don't want to live as Sheep or by Sheep rules, and they despise the Sheep. Their only goal is to wreak havoc upon the Sheep. They enjoy disturbing the peace and feel wronged by the Sheep . . . they blame the Sheep for all of their troubles and refuse to take responsibility for their own actions. Basically, they make the world unsafe for the law-abiding Sheep because they are not afraid to use violence as a means to an end.

And then there are Sheep Dogs. These are the people who protect the Sheep from the Wolves. They stand for justice, righteousness, and all that is good. Sheep Dogs hate what the Wolves stand for and are dedicated to stopping them at all costs, no matter the price, because in the end they understand if they don't take a stand, nobody else will.

Although Sheep Dogs may seem like the complete opposite of the Wolf, they are actually very similar, and therein lies the problem. In order to beat the Wolf, the Sheep Dog needs to think and act like the Wolf. Meaning Sheep Dogs are also a bit rebellious; they don't really fit in with Sheep, and they don't mind getting a bit dirty, just like the Wolves. The difference is the Sheep Dog uses his or her skills for good, where the Wolf uses them for evil.

REDEMPTION OF A COUNTERSPY

Still, Sheep Dogs are not always revered by the Sheep they protect. The Sheep often consider the Sheep Dog a necessary but ugly animal, one they don't really care to associate with because slaying Wolves is a dirty business. This reminds me of an old meme I once saw on social media. It read, "Everyone wants to be a gangster, until it's time to do gangster s*#%t!" Sheep would rather go about their business blind to the very necessary acts of violence Sheep Dogs employ on their behalf.

Grossman put it in even simpler terms. He indicated if you have no capacity for violence, then you are a healthy productive citizen, a Sheep. If you have a capacity for violence and no empathy for your fellow citizens, then you can be defined as an aggressive sociopath, a Wolf. But what if you have a capacity for violence, and a deep love for your fellow citizens? What are you then? The answer is, a Sheep Dog . . . a warrior, someone who is willing to walk the hero's path. Someone who can walk into the heart of darkness, into the universal human phobia, and walk out unscathed.

However, Grossman never talks about the very necessary Shepherd. The Shepherd is the fourth character in this story. In the Bible, human beings are referred to as sheep over 400 times. This is an interesting metaphor to use for human beings. Think about how sheep like to run off. They get lost. And even though they seem clean from a distance, they are full of nasty bugs and worms. They often get hurt and sick. They are stupid animals who are not mindful of what they eat. They require a lot of attention. That's why they need shepherds to herd and maintain them. Human beings are spiritual sheep. We lose our way, we need tending to, we eat unhealthy things, and we can be our own worst enemy. This is why Jesus is our spiritual shepherd. You may have shepherds here on earth, like parents, teachers, coaches, and mentors. That's good, but sometimes those people prove to be false shepherds, or they fail, because they are human beings in a fallen world. But Jesus, He is our way-maker. He can direct our lives if we just allow Him to shepherd us. Jesus said He was the good shepherd. And when the wolf comes growling (as sin inevitably will), Jesus does not turn and run away, He does not leave you alone to face the wolf. No, not at all. Jesus, as our Shepherd, stands between the Wolf and the Sheep (including the Sheep Dog). I never realized this until I was much older. I only knew I needed to be a Sheep Dog, but a Sheep Dog without a Shepherd is really just a wild dog. Have you sought out your master, your Shepherd?

I took an oath when I joined the Army to defend the constitution, but for me it goes much deeper than that. And I would assert it does for all who consider themselves Sheep Dogs. For us, it means we will not standby and do nothing while evil targets the innocent or those who can't protect themselves. We despise bullies in all forms and from all walks of life. If I am in a mall and an active shooter begins killing people, I will run toward the sound of gunfire. That's what I do. That's what Sheep Dogs do. That's what warriors do. We cannot stand idly by and allow evil to succeed. When Eve took a bite of the apple while Adam stood by and then eventually participated, God blamed Adam because he was responsible as the spiritual headship. If you are a man reading this, would your family say you are the spiritual headship of your family? Or would they say your wife is? If the latter, how will you rectify this?

On July 20th, 2012 during a showing of one of the Batman movies in Aurora, Colorado, an active shooter began randomly killing people in the theater. Three young teenage couples were in there watching the movie. All three girls survived, and all three boys died. Why? Because the boys used their bodies to shield the girls from the bullets the deranged killer was firing toward them. In the end, twelve people lie dead and seventy others were injured. Men are created by God to be the protectors, especially in the face of evil. As image bearers, it was in those boys' DNA to protect their girlfriends. It doesn't mean women can't or won't, but men absolutely should. We are the spiritual headship; this comes with serious responsibilities that matter for eternity.

After God created human beings and gave us dominion over the earth and over all the animal kingdom, He saw what He had created and said it was VERY good (Genesis 1:31). We are His prized possession, and every one of us has a purpose for His glory. Men have a significant role to play in this regard, and so do women! Neither of us should ignore that calling in our hearts, that little voice in our head that urges us to take a leap of faith and obey the call to share the good news of the bible with as many people as possible. Or at the very least to live your life as an example to non-Christians, demonstrating through your actions and the way you live what it means to walk with Jesus Christ.

Being a Sheep Dog means you go places Sheep do not and do what Sheep either cannot or will not do. I have seen man's inhumanity toward man, first-hand. In one certain country, I found myself in the middle of a riot during the protest of the U.S. military presence there, where a Molotov cocktail caught my suit coat on fire, burning the back of my hair and neck as well. I was fortunate I wasn't burned alive!

While following a spy through a certain foreign city, I wound up in a fight with skinheads (again) who were white supremacist. I was simply walking near a pub district when a couple of drunk skinheads saw me, decided I had to die, and jumped me. I could not even understand what they were yelling at me!

While trudging through the jungles of Latin America, I came across a dead man strapped with barbed wire to a tree, with a Colombian necktie, meaning the throat was cut with the tongue pulled through it. It was a message to would-be snitches to keep their mouths shut about information related to the cartel. The image was burned into my head, and I remember having bad dreams about that incident for months.

While in Haiti, three of us were riding in a truck when we saw a man begin to beat a defenseless woman with a stick. She fell over, and he continued to beat her in the head, face, and body. I moved to intervene, but the ranking officer in the vehicle ordered me to stand down. I was tormented in hindsight, second guessing my decision to follow orders.

When I was assigned to Panama, I once showed up unannounced at my buddy Johnny Moncada's house. He and his wife had guests over for dinner when I knocked on their door with a bloody face. I had just been jumped by two guys just down the street from Johnny's house outside of a night club. They were drunk, I was invincible, words were exchanged, and before I knew it I was fighting both men when I saw red and blue flashing lights coming toward the club, so I ran to Johnny's house.

In another country, I witnessed a man stick a knife in another man's throat while tied to a chair. I watched it happen from afar and using technical aids, but it was brutal. The man never cried out, he just scrunched his face in what I imagine was severe pain, jerked around a bit as the knife penetrated, and eventually slumped over as he bled out.

In Colombia, I stood at an intersection in Bogota waiting to cross the street when a homeless man tried to stab me with a pen for no apparent reason. The pen penetrated my leather jacket, but not the shirt beneath it and much less my skin. I took him down in one swift move, but then came to the conclusion he was mentally ill and let him go.

I became known for attracting trouble. Other CI Agents began calling me "Action Jackson" or "Sammy the Bull." I did not go out looking for trouble, trouble would always just find me! For example, in one certain country I was at the airport minding my own business when two thugs jumped me and tried to steal my briefcase I was holding, which contained classified information. I managed to fight them both off and got away with minor injuries.

Another time, different place, I was simply walking down the street in the middle of the night in a tourist area when three guys jumped out of a vehicle, one of them pointing a shotgun at me while the others tried to steal my wallet. Again, I somehow managed to fight them off, and I ended up holding the shotgun when the police arrived. The three had fled the scene just prior to that, so the cops didn't know what had happened and drew their weapons on me. My face was covered in blood, as was most of my shirt. There I stood holding a shotgun, being told to drop it and get on the ground by the cops. I did as I was told and eventually everything worked out in my favor, but wow, what a night!

In yet another country, I had just dropped off some people from the local American Embassy at the airport when I noticed a white Nissan truck with an extended cab tailgating me. I slowed down some to let it pass on my right side. As it did, out of my peripheral I noticed the truck slow down to match my speed. When I turned to look at it, in the rear left seat I noticed a man pointing a rifle right at me. I instinctively went into automatic. My left hand jerked the steering wheel to the left, hard. Thank God I was entering an intersection at the time, giving me room to turn left. At the same time, I down shifted with my right hand as my left went for my pistol. All the while ducking down just enough to see over the hood of the rental car. I remember bracing myself for a barrage of automatic gunfire to come slamming into the back windshield. But nothing happened. I continued to accelerate, now ready to fire on anyone with a gun. I looked in the rear-view mirror and saw nothing there, they must have gone straight at the intersection. We later surmised a specific group of individuals were out to kill an American, had seen me dropping off Americans at the airport, and decided to try their luck.

Then one day while living in the U.S., men from missions past came looking for me. Not good men, bad guys. They had somehow compromised my location at the time and became a threat to my family and me. It was a rare occurrence, from what I was told by my superiors, but nevertheless the threat was real. So much so that I was packed up and moved out of country within four days. I ran from the threat, something I vowed never to do again. It went against my very nature; I am a Sheep Dog, and Sheep Dogs don't run from the Wolf! But I had a family to think about. It drove me to be hyper vigilant everywhere I went. To take nothing for granted, always watch my six, and trust no one. I became the best marksman I could with pistols and rifles, and I learned formal fighting techniques from different sources, even though I could already hold my own pretty well in a fist fight. I wanted to make sure I did everything I could to be able to protect my family and me. I even trained my kids to be more vigilant. My wife and four boys learned about rally points, escape and evasion routes, and observation skills. I left nothing to chance.

I have been shot at by kids, no older than thirteen years old. I have gotten into fights simply because I was an American and a target of opportunity. I have seen a man executed in the middle of a city street; shot in the head while on his knees and while his wife and kid looked on. I have seen men do disgustingly violent things to one another, and to women and children as well. Like I said, I have personally witnessed man's inhumanity toward man. Evil truly walks upright in this world. I would later come to understand our fight is really not against the flesh. Ephesians 6:12 says our struggle is not against the flesh and blood, but against the rulers, against the authorities, against the powers of this dark world, and against the spiritual forces of evil in the heavenly realms.

What exactly does this mean? It means we live in a fallen world. And while we are here, the devil and his demons run around trying to wreak havoc in an effort to turn people, God's image bearers, away from God. It is up to us to give our hearts to Jesus and seek God through Jesus, who died on the cross for our sins and thus made it possible for us to have a relationship with God. We have a God who actually wants to be in relation with us, on a deep, personal level. No other religion in the world lays claim to such a God except for Christianity.

I wish I had understood this back then, but the truth of the matter is I simply did not. It would not be until much, much later in life that I learned what this verse meant, and it gave me a whole new perspective on people and those who commit violent acts on others. Regardless, the Wolf is always going to exist. This is understood in Christianity. He will exist until our Lord and

Savior, Jesus Christ, returns in all His glory to set things right. Until then, Sheep Dogs are necessary. They are really God's instruments in this world, for good.

If you're dealing with PTSD, perhaps you have forgotten that you are, or at the very least once were, a Sheep Dog. But at what point does the Sheep Dog begin to act more like the Wolf? I assert it happens when he spends too much time chasing after the Wolf. When he sees the Wolf eating the Sheep way too many times. Especially when he has a hard time catching the Wolf. Or when the Wolf gets away with eating too many Sheep for far too long. Maybe the Sheep Dog begins to spend too much time thinking about why the Wolf gets away with so much. Why do good Sheep get eaten? Why does our Shepherd allow so many Wolves to eat so many Sheep? Why does our Shepherd allow the existence of the Wolf? Pondering these questions without a solid spiritual foundation began to haunt me and cause my Sheep Dog to begin to retreat from the Shepherd to a corner of my inner being, avoiding ever coming out. Has this been your experience? If so, you have to get him back out by going to the Shepherd. He is in there, inside of you. He can order the Sheep Dog out and still use him for good. But if you don't get him out soon enough, you might begin slipping into darkness without the Shepherd. And if you're not careful, if you don't make a deliberate effort to bring your Sheep Dog out of that darkness, it could prove catastrophic.

I have not even begun to share with you half of what I have experienced. Because all the examples provided prior to now have been outside of a combat zone. The atrocities I witnessed there were far worse, some of them I will never speak of because they are simply too gross, disgusting, and ugly to repeat. But nonetheless, my faith in humanity to this point had been shaken. I had no idea just how much further it would be tested. In fact, it would eventually cause me to snap. Because a Sheep Dog without a Shepherd to train and guide him, to discipline him, is just a wild dog that ends up thinking and acting more like a wolf. That was what began happening to me.

6
GOD, WHERE ARE YOU?

> *"When anguish comes, they will seek peace, but there shall be none." – Ezekiel 7:25*

11 SEPTEMBER 2001. One of the worst days in American history. I was talking with Major Joe King in the hallway of our office building following a briefing from a lady from the State Department on Ukraine. Our heads were still spinning with all the social, political data this lady had filled them with. Joe was a Special Forces Major who had recently arrived at the Defense Threat Reduction Agency and was filling the shoes of an Arms Control Deputy Team Chief. I had just finished telling Joe that I'd recently spoken to some of his old buddies from the 7th Special Forces Group, back in Puerto Rico the day before. It was approximately 3 pm in Rhein-Mein Air Base, Frankfurt, Germany, where I was stationed at the time.

Gabe Amores, our office administrator came into the hallway and said, "Sam, a plane just crashed into the World Trade Center!"

Joe and I followed him through the cipher locked door into our office, where Gabe had CNN on the television. The scene was of a smoking skyscraper on a clear blue sky in New York. Just then, another plane entered the screen from the right, banked slightly to its left, and then slammed into the other World Trade Center building, causing a ball of fire and debris to explode out of the opposite side. The commentator's voice went up an octane, as he dove into a vivid description of what had just happened.

At that moment, I made a comment to the room. "That had to be deliberate," I said.

"Yeah. That was an attack," Joe replied.

And thus began the War on Terror. Soon I would find myself in various locations throughout the Middle East. I often served as a member of the U.S. Army Special Operations community. Something I totally cherished because warriors specialize in the art of war. However, let me make one thing perfectly clear: true warriors never pray for war; yet that is their business, and therefore their place of duty when it regrettably erupts. Oh, and by the way, warriors are not there to negotiate, they are there to employ violence as a means to an end. Think about it. The implication is a mindset that you only find in Sheep Dog occupations.

As I went off in support of the War on Terror to conduct sensitive activities with both conventional and special operations forces, day by day I began to question everything my grandmothers had taught me about God. Obviously I did not have a solid spiritual foundation, despite years of attending Catholic services and, to a lesser degree, Pentecostal services. I mean, I believed in God, but the minute life got tough, the early teachings I'd had fell apart. They could not withstand the onslaught of practical doubt, and so they damaged the fabric of my weak faith. And I did not have the tools to repair the damage on my own. I simply could not believe a just God would allow the type of evil I witnessed growing up through the ranks, and then now on 9/11. I knew nothing about the peace Jesus could give me if I just accepted Him into my heart. So I would stress and worry about worldly things instead of placing all of that anxiety at His feet. Nobody had ever taught me just how to do that.

If you really want to look deep into another man's soul, just go to a war zone. Deadly combat can bring to the forefront noble or shameful acts. A noble warrior understands wars are fought to bring an end to man's inhumanity toward man. When a warrior walks with Christ, he understands how to don the full armor of God and has the strength and knowledge required to keep himself from becoming the evil he seeks to destroy.

That is easier said than done and not something I particularly excelled at. I attribute it to the fact my walk with Christ was pretty much non-existent. It proved to be mentally devastating as time went on and I had more experiences in hostile environments. Places where the line between good and evil becomes blurred. In reality, the lines are still black and white, but my ability to perceive them became a gray blur, especially in tense moments of high emotion.

For example, I once witnessed a man hurl a young boy from the top of a three-story building. In the street down below was a woman whom I surmised to be the boy's mother, crying and screaming in her native language. Although I could not understand what she was saying, I most definitely understood her tears. What would you have done?

Or as another example, take the case of a twelve-year-old girl I met. She had been kidnapped from a local village in an unnamed country and taken to an old industrial area where she was repeatedly raped and sodomized by several men. I, together with a team of warriors, walked in just as this despicable act was taking place. What would you have done?

Or how about this: you meet with the mayor of a small town and when you return in a few days, he has been tortured and hung in the town square with instructions to the town's people not to cut his body down until the Americans see it. His wife, two young daughters, and his only son having to see his body hanging there for three days before we returned. What would you have done?

It has been my experience that a man's faith is usually best measured when observing acts of cruelty, or in an angry moment. It is there when one realizes doing good or evil is a choice. This choice can be hard to discern, and if you discern incorrectly, your decision can haunt you forever. How do you reconcile making the wrong decision in circumstances like these? I did not know it at the time, but the answer is unequivocally, Jesus.

One of the many things I learned as I went around the world doing the work of the U.S. Government is that a warrior, like any other man, has the absolute power to determine what he becomes, regardless of what circumstances he may find himself in. He maintains the power to do right rather than wrong. A good friend of mine once said just like lifting weights to build muscles, one must exercise discernment to build his conscience. I realize this now, but back in the warzone I did not. And I paid the price mentally for many years.

At times, I take a look at the culture around me and feel some civilians do not realize how scary combat really can be. It is nothing like what you see in the movies or television shows, or better yet, it is definitely not like any video game. It is terrifying, but guess what? It also makes you realize just how alive you really are . . . most near-death experiences do that. In that moment when you realize that someone is actually trying to end your life, to literally kill you, all of those romantic notions of combat go by the wayside. Your new reality requires you to either hunt or be hunted.

In my humble opinion, the hardest thing about being in war is watching your buddy be killed at the hands of the enemy, yet you survived. This then implants a sense of survivor's guilt that will grip you in a bear hug for years, perhaps forever if you don't figure out how to shake it loose. The internal conflict you are experiencing can drive you mad. I questioned for years whether I could have gotten to him faster, seen him go down sooner, or simply have done anything that would have changed the deadly outcome! These experiences forge a bond with your fellow warriors that you crave upon your return home. Why? Because it is pure, it is raw, it is wholesome . . . and you will never have it again, ever.

One by one, I learned of some of my friends being killed in the War on Terror. Some of them in secret missions I cannot discuss in this book. But needless to say, good men and women died, and they were my friends. People like Ferdinand Ibabao, Brian Hazelgrove, Aaron Curtis, Myla Maravillosa, Michael Goble, Brian Black, Bill "Ryan" Owens, Mihail Golin, just to name a few, because there were countless others. *God, where are you?* I thought to myself. My faith was quickly diminishing. Too much had happened, I had witnessed too much evil to believe God existed, and because I had not really gotten to know God, I did not understand Him. I did not realize at the time that the Bible actually tells us that ". . . In the world you will have tribulation. But take heart; I have overcome the world." – John 16:33

I began to hate people in general. I was angry at them, all of them. I believe during this dark time in my life, the devil could sense I had lost my faith. Have you ever been alone in the dark, and felt an ominous presence near you but nobody was physically there? Now add an aura of evil to that presence, that had been my experience. They would squat next to me, staring at me, at times I swore I could smell their stench. They were there, in the dark, with me. I think they knew my ambient signature and were attracted to it because of their inherent need to destroy image bearers.

And so there I was, in a distant country, inside a remote compound next to a village, the demons' number one High Value Target. At first I heard my name and I thought it was from one of our men, but then came the growl, the loud, insidious growl. Only this time I didn't sit up, I opened my eyes and jerked my head toward where I thought I'd heard the growl, but there was nothing of course. Nothing but the darkness of the room. I looked toward the door, and I could vaguely make out the silhouette of one of our sentries who was on shift for one hour. With sixteen people here including myself, there was no need to post a guard for more than one hour at a time. It let our people get the optimum amount of sleep.

My name . . . I'd heard my name this time. That was different, I thought to myself. That didn't sit well with me, and I thought perhaps I was finally losing my mind. I laid there in my sleeping bag, cold. Very cold. I closed my eyes and tried to get back to sleep, but that persistent feeling that someone was sitting next to me began. I simply wanted peace, at least for the night. *This must be what it's like to have a mental breakdown*, I told myself. Yep, I was losing it.

At some point in time while I was slipping into darkness, I remember speaking to God one last time before I went to sleep. I said, "God, if you are really up there, if you exist, bring the apocalypse tonight and end this experiment called man! These people are disgusting, and they do not deserve you. None of us do. So, what are you waiting for?!"

I was mad at God. I am not sure how you can be mad at someone you no longer believe exists, perhaps deep down I never really stopped believing in Him. But I did stop talking to Him, nonetheless. In addition, I would tell myself often that there was no God. I realized many years later this was the enemy whispering lies in my ear. He whispered many things into me during those years, causing me to have seriously dark thoughts.

I began drinking more. Every time my wife and I went to a party, my goal was to get drunk. I just wanted to be numb. I can't tell you how many times my wife and I argued after a party about who was going to drive. And when I would get drunk, many times I just wanted to fight with someone. My wife was constantly telling me to calm down, sit down, turn around, walk away. So often times, I would just pick a fight with her. She would tell me I was just trying to start an argument with her, and you know what? She was right! I would bring up the dumbest things to start an argument. Things like why she didn't start the dishwasher because I can't use my favorite pan now because it's dirty. Or why did she spend money on buying herself lunch, or why was she dying her hair again, or why did she change the temperature in the house without telling me? She did not deserve any of that, and she took it like a champ. For a while anyway.

Nightmares also became a common thing for me. They were usually violent, and usually involved me trying to escape or survive some attempt to harm or kill me. This is what one particular nightmare was like. It would start off just being weird but would quickly manifest into pure terror.

I am alone in a car, parked in the middle of a grassy meadow. The sky is clear and heavenly blue; there are flowers and trees in the distance along the rolling hills. I am waiting for someone... but I don't know who. Whoever it is, they are special because I am excited and nervous at the same time.

Then I hear a woman scream, it is faint, but I hear her scream. I get out of the car and look around. There, off in the distance, by the wood line! I can see a woman in a white nightgown running toward me, screaming my name. I don't recognize her, but she is running as fast as she can... why?

Then I see them, breaking out from the wood line... one, two, three of them... dogs! They are big, black dogs, they looked like German Shepherds, but I can't be sure. They are chasing this woman who continued toward me, I can see the terror in her eyes now.

I reach for my side arm, but it isn't there. I just stand there, frozen, not by fear, but by what I don't know. I just can't move my legs. As I try, my legs seem to weigh a ton, and it takes all my might just to finally move one leg forward.

The woman is now 100 meters in front of me... who is she? She has dirty blonde hair, but I still don't recognize her. She is reaching out to me with a terrified look on her face, but I can't get to her. I scream for her to run . . . but it is no good.

The first dog leaps from behind her and knocks her over. Then all three of them begin to bite her on her arms, on her legs. I yell at them to stop, and one of them turns his head to look back at me and smiles . . . the dog literally smiled! Then all three of them turn toward me and come running at me. I still can't move.

Then they suddenly stop, right there in front of me. They stop and continue to growl and bark at me, but they won't attack me. And I am scared stiff . . . I look for the girl, but she is gone. The dogs keep barking at me, louder and louder.

Suddenly the girl is in the car behind me. She is yelling at me to get in the car, but I can't move! She keeps saying, "Please, Sam, get in the car!" There is blood on her face. I don't recognize her . . .

I begin to hear a familiar voice calling my name from nearby! I frantically look around, I deeply want to see someone I know, someone who can help! However, I don't see anyone! Is the voice coming from the wood line?

"Sam! Sam!" It's louder now! I recognize it . . . it's my wife, Tricia! Oh man, what is she doing here?! But I don't see her anywhere! The dogs are in an attack posture now, where is my wife?!

"Sammy! Calm down, you're ok! Sam!" I am convinced it is my wife's voice, but where is she?!

All of a sudden, the daylight is gone, and it is pitch dark, but I can still hear the dogs barking! A flash of light. I cannot see anything! Another flash of light, this time lingering a bit longer. Back to darkness. I can feel my heartbeat racing, my hands sweating. Another flash of light lingers a little bit longer than the last one, this time I can see a silhouette in front of me for less than a second. It startles me, and I pull away, letting out a loud scream. I instinctively cover my head with my arms as I cower like a child about to be severely beaten.

My wife's voice seems much louder now, closer, and gentle.

"Babe, it's ok. It's ok, babe. You're ok, you're having another nightmare." She comforts me.

More light . . . the silhouette is her; it is Tricia. I realize light is not flashing; it is just my eyes blinking. I feel hands on my knees as I hug them to my chest. I open my eyes again, and my wife comes into focus, her face is right in front of mine.

"You're having a bad dream, babe. You're ok." She is staring at me with a look of concern, with her hands on my knees. My heartrate begins to slow, eventually stabilizing as I realize I am in the corner of my bedroom. I am embarrassed.

I slowly regain the rest of my senses. My poor wife, how many times am I going to do this to her? There I am, walking back to my bed, embarrassed about what had just happened. It was scary for her, I know. I think how tired I am of living this way. *There is no God*, I say to myself as I try to get back to sleep.

7

THE UNIMAGINABLE

> *"Do you not know that you are God's temple and that God's Spirit dwells in you? If anyone destroys God's temple, God will destroy him. For God's temple is holy, and you are that temple."* - 1 Corinthians 3:16-17

WHEN I RETURNED FROM COMBAT, I was diagnosed with PTSD, and I flat out rejected the diagnosis. I rolled my eyes at my doctor and basically told him, "You've got the wrong guy." Because in my world, PTSD was a sign of weakness. It simply meant I needed to cowboy up, to suck it up and drive on. So I didn't tell a soul about what the doctor had told me. Not my wife, not my kids, not my parents, not my best friends, NOBODY. I thought to myself, *what the heck would they say anyway? They can't possibly understand.*

So there I was, back home and living with my secret PTSD. Maybe some of you can relate. Everything is different when you return; your entire outlook on life has changed. Some of you reading this know exactly what I mean, don't you? It is as if you are living in another dimension from the one you were just in overseas. Where your friend is screaming for you to end his life due to the excruciating pain he is experiencing as a result of being shot multiple times, where a would-be assassin surprises you from behind a door with a knife and now you are locked in a hand-to-hand fight for one last breath, or where the tormenting demons won't leave your head. Where you drink alcohol to numb the pain. Where the enemy whispers in your ear so that depression grips you in a bear hug and doesn't let go for weeks at a time. That was my new reality, and I never dared to talk about it. Did you?

I realize it can be difficult for civilians to understand the concept of one preferring to die rather than abandoning one's brother warriors in the fight. Soldiers train together for years for combat with the promise they will never leave one another behind. Survivor's guilt sets in because somehow you made it back alive instead of dying next to them. And speaking of making it back, for me, I was in such a decayed state of mind that I was actually sickened by the fact people were walking around the malls here in the homeland, caring more about lattes, skinny jeans, smart phones, barbeques, fancy cars, parties, sports, and ballgames. All the while American men and women were dying overseas! Now, this was not fair to those people, but at the time I did not care about them or their stupid desires. I hated them, I hated people. Have you ever felt that way?

My wife took notice. My PTSD became increasingly worse. To say I was in a very dark place in my life was an understatement.

The nightmares; waking up in the middle of the night out of breath and terrified. Having a panic attack in crowded places. Hearing a sound, or smelling a scent, or even just observing something that triggers the brain, taking you back to the place you never want to return to.

Anger issues, alcohol issues, relationship issues . . . it all came to a head in October of 2015 when my wife said to me, "You're not the man I married. I'm not sure I can live with you anymore." That was a slap in the face and a wakeup call for me. It caused me to look in the mirror. I didn't like what I saw, but I didn't know how to fix it.

I had not accepted any drugs from the docs for my PTSD, so I considered going back and asking for those. I considered therapy and counseling. But that meant I had to admit I had a problem first. I had to face my demons. That simply was not an option for me at the time. I was just not ready. And so I was paralyzed. In the meantime, SFC Peter Engelking deliberately overdosed himself. MAJ Brian Kavanagh shot himself. LTC Kelly Hodge hung himself. And Chief Warrant Officer Gerry Cole shot himself with a crossbow in the heart. All of them suffering from PTSD. All of them were my friends. And then, with my faith now completely gone, I too considered the unimaginable.

In the late summer of 2016, the world seemed to be caving in on me, even though I had previously come clean about my PTSD and was working towards better health. My marriage was falling apart. My PSTD was getting worse. I would lose my temper easily. The road rage was uncontrollable; I came very close to shooting a truck driver once for driving too slow in the passing lane. I was drinking more heavily. The arguments with my wife about wanting to drive home after a night of drinking at a friend's house or at a bar, even though I was clearly not in any condition to drive, were getting much worse. The nightmares were now nonstop. I was also deeply depressed, to the point I found it very hard to get out of bed in the morning. I felt lonely, although I was rarely alone. Loneliness can cause people to feel exhausted. In addition, although people were in fact around me, I did not feel "seen" in a sense. Because nobody knew what I was struggling with on the inside, I could not be my true self to the world. Therefore, in essence, I was unseen, my true self was unseen. Have you ever felt lonely in a sea of people?

Additionally, my physical health was in the worst shape ever; I was battling several illnesses such as high blood pressure, high cholesterol, and diabetes, to name a few. I was tipping the scales as far as my weight, and I was always irritable, strike that, I was angry . . . with everyone . . . about everything. Perhaps one of the reasons I was so angry is because I had become impotent, unable to have an erection. This was playing out very badly in my marriage because my wife felt I no longer found her sexually attractive. I did not understand why this was happening and refused to take any pills for it. I was much too young to be having these issues. As I would initiate an intimate moment with my wife, she would become aroused. But I just could not rise to the occasion, leaving my wife frustrated and hurt because she thought it was because of her that I could not get aroused. Eventually she completely stopped being intimate with me in any way. That did a lot of damage to our marriage. Making love to your spouse is important. Married couples are supposed to have sex, to make love to each other. A loss of intimacy begins a downward spiral that drives a wedge between couples. That was what was happening in my marriage, and I couldn't stop it. I began looking at other couples with envy. Jealousy would swell up inside of me anytime I saw another couple holding hands or just being loving toward each other, because I no longer had that. Of course, I realized those couples may possibly have had issues in their marriage I did not know about, but I didn't care. The fact they were being affectionate with one another in public caused me great pain. My wife was no longer interested in being affectionate with an angry, impotent man. I was hurting inside. My marriage was dying. My very soul was aching.

The news also did not help. I would see something in the news that would make me angry to the point I would dwell on it for days. I would get mad and yell at the television as if I were watching a football game and my team was losing. My wife would get startled and then tell me to shut up or to stop screaming. I would then fire back with some mean or rude comment and that would trigger an argument with her. Suffice it to say, I was not a pleasant person to be around.

Oh, and did I mention I hated people? Yeah, like I really despised human beings. After having been deployed to some of the worst places on the planet and bearing witness to man's inhumanity toward man year after year, I kept saying to myself that evil really does walk upright in this world. Often times when I looked at another human being, I saw an animal that needed to be slaughtered. Dark images of how I could slaughter them would enter my mind. I would actually become disgusted with someone I was having a conversation with right in the middle of the conversation, and my mind would drift to those dark thoughts and images. How many of you have experienced this? Does it still happen?

Often times I would judge other people and talk bad about

them. I felt people were just stupid and disgusting. More and more, I found less and less people I cared to associate with. About the only people I enjoyed being around anymore were my sons and my parents. Since I felt my wife did not like being around me anymore, I was beginning to consider her a lost cause. That would keep me awake at night because deep inside I still loved her. But the enemy was winning the fight for my mind through my heart. The enemy knew exactly how to drive a wedge between Tricia and me. He has been doing it in marriages around the world since the beginning. Without any faith on my part, it was becoming easier and easier for him to creep into our marriage and continue to plant seeds of despair, anguish, and heartbreak. That's what he does. Does any of this sound familiar to you?

My father works at Brook Army Medical Center on Fort Sam Houston as an IT specialist. I will go have lunch with him frequently. On one particular occasion, we had just finished lunch and I was on my way toward the hospital exit. I got in an elevator and then my memory blacked out. Next thing I knew, I was walking around the parking lot looking for my car. I could not find my car. So I went back inside to retrace my steps and it was then I realized I had come out of the wrong door. I was parked on the other side of the hospital! I exited the opposite side and found my car. A few weeks later I was trying to figure out why I had a block of missing time in my memory. I asked myself what happened in that elevator that I could not remember. Then it finally hit me. My memory came back, bits at a time at first, then the full memory. While in the elevator, it stopped at another floor and two women in Islamic head garb entered the elevator. Now, remember how I said I hated people, well I hated Muslims even more. Muslims had killed many of my friends and were responsible for 9/11. They deserved nothing but death. That was what I felt like then, but Jesus would later change my heart completely. More on that later.

Back to the elevator. When they got inside the elevator and as a result were in such very close proximity to me, I lost it. I wanted to hurt them. I became instantly angry, and all kinds of crazy thoughts went through my mind, again, dark thoughts. We all exited the elevator together but I, in my furious state of mind, did not realize I was walking toward the opposite exit from where I had entered. Perhaps I was just trying to remove myself quickly from their presence, I don't know. But I truly believe the enemy wanted me to hurt those women, and just imagine if I had done it. I was truly in need of help.

In fact, I remember my son Jesse, coming home late one night from one of his tours in Afghanistan. I picked him up at the airport at around 11 pm, then we went home and sat in the living room for a while talking about his experiences in combat, then mine. I said some dark things, and once he realized I was harboring deep, angry feelings, he said something to me that rocked me on my heels. He looked at me in the eye and said, "Dad, you need professional help." My immediate reaction was one of shock. *Did my son really just say that to me?* I thought. *Why would he say that? Surely he didn't mean it. I mean, I don't need any help. I'm good.* I wasn't good, and my son knew it.

Now, at this point you might be asking yourself why I did not just talk to one of my warrior friends. Well, there is a paradigm that exists among warriors that sometimes makes it challenging for them to be vulnerable with one another. For those dealing with issues of PTSD, it creates a roadblock to true healing, because one warrior may refuse to confide in another due to fears of what that warrior may think. Often times we place our most trusted warrior friends on such a high pedestal we fear being viewed by them as soft or mentally weak. Does this sound familiar to you? This is not the same as having everyday friends in the civilian world that you can't confide in for fear of what they may think. The difference is, in the former you have a deep admiration and respect for your warrior brethren, who holds you on an equally high pedestal, causing you to fear being viewed as anything but strong. Because warriors are not supposed to be weak.

For almost a year, I walked around with the enemy whispering in my ear that I should take my own life. At work, nobody knew what was going on. I smiled, held conversations, laughed, and participated in practical jokes on co-workers. I remember once a senior military officer made the comment that our office had a tendency to "joke around too much." He added, "They need to be more serious in the office." When we heard that, we burst out in laughter and continued our shenanigans! The point was my boss never had a clue. My co-workers never had a clue. My family never had a clue. Nobody had a clue about the spiritual warfare going on inside me. I did not want anybody to know. I did not want any of my colleagues to know I was a weak man, because as a man, a spy catcher, and terrorist catcher, I had to be strong. But I was hurting so bad inside. I was hurting for my friends who had been killed, for the slaughter of innocents I witnessed, for not being good enough . . . or for not being good, period. For failing as a husband, for the survivor's guilt playing out in my head. I was hurting because I was being so fake when I did not even believe in God anymore. A fake son, father, husband, friend. I guess in actuality, I hated myself. Can you relate to this feeling?

So one morning, I decided I could no longer live with this pain. I felt a heavy burden on my shoulders that was only getting heavier and darker. The enemy kept whispering in my ear that I deserved to die, I was not worthy of Heaven. That the pain would go away if I just ended my own life. The enemy convinced me I would actually be doing everyone, including my wife and kids, a favor by just ending it. That I was hurting them with my issues. So, I came up with a deliberate plan to end my life.

I had rented a hotel room, so my wife and kids did not have to live in the place where they would find my body. I would stick the gun deep in the back of my mouth, being careful to aim it toward my brain, but not too high that it blew off the top of my head, just the back of it. This way my family could still see me in an open casket. I also made sure to wear old clothes, none of my favorite shirts or pants. Just some old shorts and a t-shirt.

I wrote a suicide note apologizing to my wife, kids, and parents for not being strong enough, and trying to explain my rationale for doing the unimaginable. I remember crying so much as I wrote it. I really was so sorry, but I just felt there was no other way. I stuck the letter in an envelope along with a necklace with a cross my mom had given me before leaving for the Army. For some strange reason I did not want to do it while wearing it around my neck. I placed the envelope on the pillow behind me as I sat at the foot of the bed, believing after pulling the trigger I would fall backwards on the bed, and that was how I would be found, with the letter above my head. Then I locked and loaded my pistol, sat on the bed, and placed it in my mouth. The cold steel bumped on my upper front teeth as I moved the barrel in further, I thought to myself how the slight pain it caused would not matter in just a few seconds.

As I placed the gun in position, I closed my eyes, and my wife and parents flashed in my head. *I'm sorry, babe . . . I'm sorry mom and dad,* I thought to myself. All of them were strong, and they would be ok, I rationalized to myself. Then I began the mental countdown and placed my finger on the trigger; three . . . here it goes, two . . . wait! I relaxed my finger. "What's wrong with you?" I asked myself. "Let's go, you got this, just do it. Don't think about it, just do it. Do it now!" As I pumped myself up, I began to slowly squeeze the trigger. I closed my eyes tight and braced for the shot. I wondered if I would even feel any pain. I could feel the pressure of the trigger on my forefinger now. Any second the trigger would move and that would be it.

But then my kids flashed into my mind and my finger came off the trigger, my eyes wide open. *My kids, what would they think?* Well, for one that Dad was not Superman after all. *Would they be mad at me? Would they become dysfunctional as they grew up knowing their dad was weak and killed himself?* The thoughts lingered. And then slowly, I pulled the gun from my mouth, dropped it on the bed, fell to the carpet floor, and curled up in the fetal position, crying profusely and then becoming angry at myself for not being able to go through with it. It remains the lowest point in my life to this day.

And nobody knew. Nobody was the wiser. *Well, I can still give it another try later,* I thought to myself.

PART THREE
FOUND PEOPLE WHO FIND PEOPLE

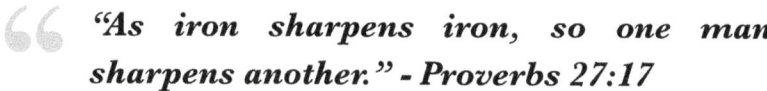

8
THE POWER OF ONE

> *"As iron sharpens iron, so one man sharpens another." - Proverbs 27:17*

IN 2015, prior to my suicide attempt, my wife had approached me about taking some capsules one of her friends had recently told her about.

"What's in them?" I asked her as she shoved these capsules in front of me.

"They say they are just salads in a capsule. They have fruits and vegetable nutrients in them, so they are healthy for you," she explained.

"I'm not going to fail my urinalysis, am I?" I asked. Having a security clearance meant submitting to random drug testing and I did not want to put anything in my system that might jeopardize my clearance. Because without my security clearance, I could not maintain my government job.

"It's just fruits and veggies," she told me. "And besides, your son, Alex, doesn't like fruits and vegetables, and he can get these for free in chewable form. So lead by example and take them." My wife was an Army wife, and knew how to manipulate her Army husband, even though I was now a civilian.

Juice Plus is a company that figured out how to put fruits, vegetables, and berries in a capsule. Ever heard of it? One of my wife's friends had recently become a distributer, and my wife purchased the product since we ate very unhealthy at the time. In fact, my body was falling apart. I was seriously overweight and on eight different prescription medications for high blood pressure, high cholesterol, high triglycerides, diabetes, and low potassium, to name just a few illnesses I was dealing with. To top it off, I was a couch potato, my energy was at an all-time low.

Well, lucky for me, my wife had partnered with the Juice Plus Company and she convinced me to start taking the capsules. Now, I was going to see my doctor every three months because I was in such poor health. And every time he would see me, he would reprimand me for my weight and my diet. But after just three months of being on this product, my doctor was so impressed with my blood work he told me, "Whatever you're doing, just keep doing it." So I did. And I realized I suddenly had more energy. I started going for walks in my neighborhood. Then I got back into the gym. Eight months later, I came off of ALL prescription medications and I had lost almost forty pounds! I can't promise everyone will have the same results because our bodies are all different, but I know this for a fact: everyone can benefit from more fruits and vegetables!

I was encouraged by the improvement of my physical health. My mental health was also starting to see just a tiny bit of improvement as well. And I felt I had to share this with the distributers my wife had befriended. So, one night in Phoenix, Arizona during a Juice Plus event, I got up in front of about fifty or so Juice Plus representatives and my wife, and for the first time ever, I verbalized the fact I was battling PTSD. And furthermore, how Juice Plus had helped me improve my physical and mental health. This was the first time my wife learned I was diagnosed with PTSD. I had never mentioned it to her. She told me that night that it made sense now why I was always being such a jerk, and that I should have told her sooner.

Several people came up to me afterwards to hug me and just praise me for being vulnerable in front of so many. One lady named Cathy encouraged me to continue verbalizing my story, sharing more details as I felt more comfortable doing so. That it was therapeutic to do so. Another newfound friend, Jacqi, came up to me and asked if she could hug me. It remains one of the best hugs I have ever gotten from a friend. And yet another young lady, Rachael, simply came up and placed her hand on my shoulder, rubbed it up and down while looking at me with sympathetic eyes, and moved on without saying a word. The strength of that simple gesture was powerful. It is as if she told me with just her look, that everything was going to be ok.

While this remains one of my most memorable nights, it was not yet enough to keep the enemy at bay. He continued to whisper in my ear, even more now. I believe he did not want me around this Juice Plus team, as he understood full well the power these people wielded. Why? Because they were Christians.

On August 28th, 2016, just a couple of days after I attempted suicide, I attended a business coaching seminar in Dallas, Texas with many from my Juice Plus tribe. My wife was in Los Angeles at the time taking care of her sick mother (we were still having marriage issues despite my coming clean about my PTSD), so two of our friends who also attended the seminar with me asked me for a ride back to our home near San Antonio, Texas. Rachael and Jacqi (whom I previously met in Phoenix when I first announced I was battling PTSD), had flown up to Dallas with Jacqi's husband, who was a pilot for Southwest Airlines. It was my pleasure to give them a ride back because it is a long, four-hour drive home, and I welcomed the company.

During the ride, Rachael asked me, "What church do ya'll go to?"

Rachael DeBoy is from Lawrence, Kansas. She grew up going to church, and her faith remains unshakeable. She can light up the room with her smile, and her energy and positivity is contagious. Having worked in the finance sector for many years, Rachael left the world of trading hours for dollars to build a business with Juice Plus. It was a perfect match for her desire to do good in the world. And what could be better than helping people with their health AND their wealth. Her Juice Plus business allowed her to leave the finance industry behind and stay home with her four little ones, with the freedom to choose the people she partnered with on her mission to inspire healthy living among her friends and family and throughout her community.

I knew she maintained a strong faith, and I had never admitted to anyone that I had stopped believing in God, so I just replied with, "Well, we haven't really found one we're comfortable with."

It was then, in that moment, that God used His disciple, Rachael, to do His bidding . . . to invite me to her church.

"It's a lot of fun and very laid back, I'd love to see you there sometime," Rachael proclaimed.

I had absolutely no intention of taking her up on her invitation. In fact, I thought to myself how naive she was for believing a God could even exist, and how she too would not believe in God if she had seen what I had seen, experienced what I had experienced. But little did I know Rachael's invitation was a divine intervention; it was not by accident she had gotten into my car that hot summer Texas day, although I did not realize it then.

After I dropped Rachael and Jacqi off at their homes, I went to mine and did not give going to church a second thought. At least not until the very next Sunday morning, that is. I'm an early riser to begin with, and that Sunday was no exception. However, on this particular Sunday I felt a peculiar calling in my heart; I was feeling compelled to go to church. Rachael's previous conversation with me replayed in my mind. "You should come to my church," she had said to me. I decided I would go take a look; it may be interesting to see what load of crap they are feeding the Sheep these days in that building they call church. It was how I felt, but little did I know it was the Holy Spirit that had compelled me to go to church that day, and for whatever reason, I was ready, although I did not know it yet. I did not know my heart was actually ready to take the leap of faith; it was all happening without my realizing it. I was just sort of going with the flow.

Everyday Christian Fellowship Church is a non-denominational church in our small town of Cibolo, Texas. It is nothing fancy, resembling more a warehouse than a church with its tin roof and metal siding. Inside, service takes place on a gym floor with basketball hoops on each side. People sit on individual chairs that are neatly stacked following service as other events take place during the week requiring the space. It is a casual setting to say the least, with a diverse congregation. Some folks wear their Sunday best, while others show up in t-shirts and flip-flops, and nobody judges them. I have come to learn Jesus doesn't care what you wear to church, as long as you show up! Rachael would later say to me concerning the church congregation that we are all "-just a bunch of messed up people doing life together!" A perspective I have shared with others so often.

As I walked in, I was greeted by a friendly member of the church staff who welcomed me and made me feel instantly comfortable. Still, I sat in the very back left corner of the church. As far away from the pastor as I could get. Even though I no longer believed in God, having been raised Catholic, I felt uncomfortable being in a non-Catholic church ... strange, I know. I really do not recall what went through my mind sitting there initially, but I remember how I felt. I felt a bit awkward, yet peaceful.

The pastor began talking about guilt, and how some believe they are not worthy of Heaven, two issues I had been dealing with as of late! As he continued talking about asking Christ to come into your life and surrendering all to Him, I felt as if he was speaking directly to me! The feeling was followed by a sudden rush of emotions overwhelming me at my core. Then I felt a strange sense of confusion, as if I could not believe how relatable the pastor's message was to me. I was captivated, no, mesmerized is a better word, by his message of hope and deliverance! My heart began to race, my breathing was shallow and quick, my hands began to fidget! And then I could no longer hold back; I began to weep. And as my tears flowed uncontrollably from my body, so too did any reservations about being in church, even a non-Catholic one.

When the service ended, I stood up and prepared to depart when I noticed Rachael making her way through the crowd toward me. As our eyes met, I could tell she was surprised to see me, her face wearing that million-dollar smile.

When she arrived to where I was standing, she said in a rather surprised manner, "Sammy! You came to church!"

I sort of laughed as I said, "Yeah, well, you invited me!"

We talked briefly about the sermon, and I promised her I would definitely be back the following Sunday. Although I felt like the sun's rays had just broken through the dark, stormy clouds, I had no idea the enemy does not give up that easily and serious battles were yet to come.

I went home that day, walked into my walk-in closet, fell to my knees, arms stretched up high, and with a crying voice, I said, "Ok God, here I am! I give up! Please help me, because I don't know how to do this! I am at the end of my rope, and I don't know what to do anymore! If you're up there, please make this pain in my soul go away! I am so sorry, please do not leave me! Please help!" Have you tried this? Do you believe it can help?

Following that Sunday service, I remember asking Rachael if she would be my "Spiritual Mentor." She agreed and immediately had me download the Bible App. I do not know why the fact a Bible App existed came as a surprise to me, as there are apps for literally everything nowadays, but it did. I did as she instructed and began to read the Bible using the app's Bible plans.

For the next week, I was like a sponge, reading the Bible and soaking up everything I could. I had so many questions for Rachael, who very lovingly and patiently answered all of my questions. During one Sunday service, the pastor explained what it takes to be saved. I was sitting next to Rachael, so I leaned toward her and whispered, "That seems so simple. Is it really that simple?"

She replied, "Yes, but you have to believe with all your heart because God knows what is on your heart!"

On September 18th, 2016, I told God I believe in His Son, Jesus. That Jesus died on the cross for my salvation. That I repented of my sins, and that I believed Jesus rose from the dead and ascended into Heaven. I made the decision in my heart to follow Jesus Christ for the rest of my life. I meant every word of it. I was saved. Almost immediately I could feel a heaviness I had battled begin to subside. The depression went from coming at me for weeks at a time, to just days (and then eventually minutes). I felt truly born again and free in a way I had never experienced!

Soon thereafter, Rachael asked me if I had ever been baptized. Of course I had, as I previously mentioned I was raised Catholic and as such I was baptized at birth. But she was asking me if I had ever been baptized as an adult, and I had not. So, Rachael had me sign up for the Bible plan on Baptism. It was a three-day plan explaining its biblical origins and how it is a public declaration of your decision to accept Christ into your heart and that you will follow Him.

I initially had reservations about even considering baptism, concerned about what my mother may think about this non-Catholic church baptizing her first born. But after reading through the Bible plan and believing my mother would probably not oppose too strongly, I made a decision, and on January 1st, 2017, I was baptized.

The spiritual high was overwhelming, and I couldn't get enough of it. Rachael continued to have conversations with me about God and scripture. I yearned for a deeper understanding of His word. She had locked arms with me and had brought me back to Christ. Rachael gave me perspectives and insights I truly valued, and her knowledge and understanding of the Gospel was and continues to be impressive to this day. I would observe her mannerisms and dealings with others. She is a great example of how human beings should interact with one another. Even when she is frustrated or angry, she speaks from a place of love. She taught me to pray right away when you need to talk to God or ask for His help or blessings. "There is no need to wait," she would tell me. "Just close your eyes and bow your head right there and then and talk to God. He is listening."

But suddenly, and I do mean suddenly, the enemy struck back with an all-out counter-offensive with depression, leading an assault on my mind and soul. It was then I learned spiritual warfare is a very real thing, and when you are growing closer to Christ, the enemy hones in on you and deliberately targets you for attack. This made sense to me, I mean, why would he not? He wants your soul; he aims to make you miserable so you will indulge in all manners of vice and depravity. In my humble opinion, man as he is constituted is weak without God and prone to lying, cheating, stealing, and all manners of debauchery. The enemy knows this and does what he can to keep you from walking with Christ. This is why it is so important to watch the company you keep! Like my dad used to say to me when I was a kid, if you want to be a winner, hang out with winners. If you want to be a loser, hang out with losers. Some of the wisest words he ever spoke to me that can be applied to so many different contexts.

Back to my depression. This time I saw it coming, I could feel it creeping in at the onset, so I was able to reach out to Rachael for counsel as it tore into my heart. She very wisely advised me to invoke the authority of Jesus Christ out loud over the enemy's whispers in my ear, and it worked. But the enemy wasn't finished with me yet.

The enemy's assaults continued over the ensuing months, with Rachael advising me to recite certain scriptures in the heat of the battle. The enemy would retreat and then come back even stronger. It was then that Rachael suggested listening to Christian music to help repel the attacks. Now, I love music. All types of genres, but I had never, ever sat and listened to Christian music. Rachael explained I should focus on the words and treat it as a time to worship while I listened and even sang the words out loud. So I did as she instructed. And guess what? Yep, it worked. The combination of invoking Jesus' name, reciting scripture, and singing Christian songs was a strong arsenal against my determined enemy! Have you ever tried this?

You never know what a person is struggling with on the inside. Rachael knew when she met me I was dealing with PTSD, but she later admitted it was not until after getting to know me a little bit that she realized how real this issue is for people. Her strong faith in Jesus Christ led her to be obedient to God's will. He used her, worked through her to help me. Because she listened to Him and locked arms with me, my thoughts of suicide vanished. She literally saved my life.

Rachael later said to me after I thanked her for saving my life that she did not feel like she had done anything for me at all. That is just pure, raw humility of the highest kind! Her relationship with God is such that she does not often even realize those moments when He is using her for His glory! I often wonder what would have happened to me had she not invited me to her church. What if she had not invested time and energy in me at all? What if she had been selfish and said to herself, "Oh he'll be fine. I am a busy woman, I don't have time to give him and besides, I hardly know him." I may very well be divorced and perhaps even dead. But I am still here, still alive. All because ONE person cared. That is all it takes, just for ONE person to care! Imagine how beautiful this world could be if we all made it a point to be that ONE person for someone else! Do you have someone like Rachael in your life? Are you that ONE person to someone else, perhaps?

How do I know Rachael coming into my life was divine intervention? Because we are both married. In the beginning of our relationship we spent a lot of time together socially, if her husband or my wife were jealous people it never would have worked out. God knew exactly who was up for the task of bringing me back to Him. My guess is He probably "told" other men to help but they did not "listen," they were not obedient. So He sent a woman to do a man's job, and she did it perfectly.

Now, do you remember at the beginning of this book when I talked about being in Iraq and how the old man who spoke Aramaic told me I would meet a blonde woman and she would save my soul? I now realize he was talking about Rachael; she was prophesied to me way back then, before the real struggle had even begun. How cool is that?! At first my mind kept dismissing this realization as superstitious nonsense, but Rachael's wise words once again grounded me and allowed me to believe when she said to me, "The Bible is full of stories about prophesying, and you do believe the Bible, right?" There was no arguing with that!

But before you go giving Rachael all the credit, you must know she had help! You see, Rachael was that one person who reached out to me and, through her spiritual mentorship and perspectives, facilitated my understanding of the tribe I had just been introduced to. As if blinders had been shattered, my heart, mind, and soul were now ready to see the world through a completely different lens! One of love and compassion. As I looked at the world around me just like a newborn seeing the world for the first time, I observed the tribe in its truest form. The tribe had gone from being just a bunch of people I referred to as the Juice Plus, Shooting Stars Team or Juice Plus representatives, to seeing them as a tribe of like-minded people with a genuine concern for the plight and circumstances of others, rooted in a deep and unyielding faith. Like the song "Amazing Grace" says, "I once was blind, but now I see." Well, I saw alright, and I was about to see even clearer than ever before.

9
SHOOTING STARS

> *"But you are a chosen race, a royal priesthood, a holy nation, a people for his own possession, that you may proclaim the excellencies of him who called you out of darkness into his marvelous light." – 1 Peter 2:9*

WHEN I FIRST MET THE Juice Plus tribe, I thought they were all fake. I thought to myself, *there is no way people can be so happy, positive, and encouraging all the time.* But they were. Each new representative of the Juice Plus company I met displayed the same loving attributes. However, what I did not realize at the time was the fact most of the one's I had met were Christians. And the team of Juice Plus reps that my wife found herself on when she signed up to be a partner were known as the Shooting Stars.

At first, my wife did not want to introduce me to them. Every time they had an event, Tricia would say it was just for women or just for the representatives. Later I would come to find out they had become Tricia's safe space. It was where she went to get away from me. She is a cancer survivor and one of the most resilient women I have ever met right alongside my mother. As a cancer survivor, she had made up her mind she needed to limit negativity, and the Shooting Stars were her escape. Much later, after I was saved, it would take a while to come to terms with the change I was experiencing. It had come too fast, and being that I had put Tricia through hell for so many years before coming to Christ, it was hard for her to quickly let down the defenses it had taken her years to build. It would take time and getting used to the new me. Have you ever experienced this?

Before I was saved, I pulled up to our friend, Lori's house to drop off my wife for a team meeting with her newfound Juice Plus friends. Standing in the driveway were Lori and her best friend, Danette. Danette was a country girl who grew up on a farm in Illinois with a very conservative Christian upbringing. She eventually met and married her husband, who went on to become an Air Force fighter pilot. For many years, Danette lived a very self-imposed, strict life as a wife. In her eyes, it was not good for married women to have male friends, so she did not. She basically believed a women's place was in the home. To cook, clean, and have children. To support their husbands and never question their authority as men, as head of the household. Well, after partnering with the Juice Plus company, Danette began to question everything she believed about being a woman in today's world. She saw other women transforming themselves into powerful women with the confidence to succeed at their own home businesses, some of whom even retired their husbands from whatever careers they had. These women are out there showing other women how they can also have the time and finances to make a life, not just a living. Within the Juice Plus company, many refer to their home business as a self-development course disguised as a business. Danette was learning new things, but at the time still had a bit further to go.

Seeing Lori and Danette in the driveway, I pulled up near them and rolled down my window. My wife greeted them from the passenger side and introduced me as her husband. Lori was closest to my side of the car, and Danette stood a ways back behind her. Danette did not approach any closer. She would later confess to me that I "looked scary." She said there was a darkness about me she couldn't quite explain, so she kept her distance. The enemy was constantly whispering in my ear during those days, and I truly believe it wasn't necessarily how I appeared physically that scared Danette (ok, perhaps debatable), I believe her divine sensors were simply set off at the presence of my darkness (I had not yet been saved when I first met her). It was a case of good meets evil.

Years later, Danette would transform herself into a powerful public speaker, advocating for women to live their best life through a process of self-development that included Jesus Christ. It was then she apologized to me for judging me that first day we met. Following her confession (which was totally unnecessary as far as I was concerned), we became close friends and remain so to this day. Like Rachael, Danette knows Jesus very well and I personally believe both of them have a special place reserved for them in Heaven. Do you know anyone like that?

But at the time I met her and the rest of the Juice Plus tribe, I was struggling to understand why they were so good to one another, as well as to others. I have never met so many people who genuinely and sincerely want the best for each other. They are not in competition with each other. They do not look at each other's clothes, cars, homes, or other worldly possessions with envy. They lift each other up constantly and help each other out whenever someone is in need of anything. And most importantly, they love unconditionally. I realized quickly their encouraging, loving positivity was just what I needed. I needed a tribe just like this one. Because we are relational beings, created by God to be relational. More about that later.

Shortly after meeting the Shooting Stars team and coming clean about my battle with PTSD, one of the ladies on the team, Sarah Jonsgaard and her husband, Erik, sent me a DVD. My wife and I had previously met Sarah in Phoenix when I revealed I was struggling with PTSD. I later met Erik at a Juice Plus summit in Dallas, Texas. They had learned that with the support of my wife, I was now doing some work with veterans (we will get to that later) and decided to send me a DVD titled, "Taking the Hill: A Warrior's Journey Home." It was about a Marine who fought in Vietnam, his name is Raul Ries. He has a very powerful story about overcoming PTSD with the help of Jesus, and he is now a pastor at Calvary Chapel Golden Springs in Diamond Bar, California. Inside the DVD case was a 3 x 5 index card with a hand-written message that read as follows:

"Hey guys,

Just wanted to share this powerful DVD with you guys. I know you are doing profound, life changing work with veterans and was hoping this might help you! Thank you for ALL you guys are doing to help those who have helped keep our families free.

The Jonsgaards"

I was so touched by this heartfelt gift. At the time, the

Jonsgaards were living in Colorado. I don't take such gestures lightly. I considered it a big deal that they mailed us this DVD all the way from Colorado and made sure I told them just how much I appreciated it.

This is the caliber of people I have found in the Shooting Stars. They simply know how to love and encourage others. They were exactly the type of people I needed to surround myself with in order to improve my mental health, especially my depression. So I began going to any conference or summit that was on the schedule. The beauty about this team is that they literally live all across the United States and love to travel! We often link up at national and regional conferences and summits in places like Los Angeles, Indianapolis, Phoenix, St. Louis, Dallas, and even San Antonio! I figured, if a small group of Shooting Stars here in the greater San Antonio area can be good for me, just imagine how good it is to hang out with all of them!

After meeting this tribe and after Jesus saved my life using Rachael, I realized my physical, mental, and spiritual health continued to improve. I began attending "Wellness Workshops." These are free, informal get-togethers where Juice Plus reps show participants simple ways to improve their health. Such as making salads in a jar, overnight oats, or even how to make kombucha. The point of the workshops besides the 'how to' is also to educate and inform participants on how important whole-food nutrition is to a healthy body, particularly the intake of plenty of fruits, vegetables, and berries.

The other thing inherent to these workshops is the social aspect, as they deliberately build community. This is where tribe members come together in a fun, positive environment to make a difference in the lives of others. To provide hope for mom's struggling with picky eaters, people with various illnesses, and for people struggling with mental health challenges, like me, for instance. I learned I had to turn off the news because it was a constant source of anger and stress for me. I had to avoid negative people (for now) and choose to be happy about life. To focus on those things that brought me joy. Being around this tribe brings me joy. My love language is physical touch (if you don't know what a love language is, look it up on Google), and this tribe is full of huggers!

Do you have negative things or people in your life that you need to remove, like the news? Maybe you are in a job that is just taking everything out of you, draining you, and leaving you frustrated, annoyed, or perhaps simply angry at the end of each day. Or perhaps you have a friend who constantly focuses on the negative, never having a positive word to say. Is it time to distance yourself from those negative relationships, at least until you get some mental healing done? Is it time to get a new job? Isn't your mental health more important than any of these things?

I ended up meeting person after person in this tribe who demonstrated the same positive gifts of the Holy Spirit, being charity, joy, peace, patience, kindness, goodness, generosity, gentleness, faithfulness, modesty, self-control, chastity. I believe that is why God has so blessed them, because they are real people, real Christians who understand the Gospel and apply it in their everyday lives. With this tribe is where I came to understand key concepts of money.

For example, part of the Juice Plus home-based business model is attracting others to the business as well, it's known as multi-level marketing (not a pyramid scheme). People who might want to earn a little (or a lot of) extra cash on the side. While watching a virtual event with the tribe, the famous rapper Pitbull came on stage as a guest of the event and said one thing that I have never forgotten. He said, "They say money doesn't buy happiness. Well, yes it does. You just gotta give it away." This concept runs rampant among the Shooting Stars.

During another training event, I don't remember who it was, but someone was talking about how crazy it is to NOT want to have a side gig. They went on to ask why someone would choose to NOT make more money. I flashed back to my mom and my grandma, who always taught me to be happy with what I have, to include when it comes to money. I realize it was a different time back in their day, there weren't a lot of opportunities for side gigs in the Arnet Benson that weren't illegal! But with today's technology, namely the internet and smart phones, one can earn serious money with the right side gig. Shooting Stars are a testament to this. What I learned that day was that EVERYONE should have a side gig, especially CHRISTIANS. Why? Because we give so much away! I personally want to make more money so I can give more to charities and causes that I personally care about. I want to help more people.

Think about it. Those of you reading this who do not have a side gig, what are some causes you are passionate about helping? Perhaps you already give some money to charities, like your church, some animal charities, homeless shelters, anti-human trafficking non-profits, children's charities, cancer research, maybe you have adopted a poor little girl in Liberia. Just think about how much more you could give to any one of those and perhaps several others if you only had a side gig. What about being able to help family and friends? Or strangers? During the holidays, I always find myself thinking, *if only I had more money, I could help more people.*

Many of you reading this right now are saying to yourselves, "I make enough money." Really? No such thing. I don't care how much money you make, you can and should always make more, especially if you are a true Christian. Because money is one of the most powerful ways to do good in this world, to alleviate pain, to end suffering, and to provide resources to those in dire need. And the more money Christians have, the more good they can do in this world.

Now I don't want to hear anything about money being the root of all evil. That is simply not true. It is the LOVE of money that is the root of all evil. You can't be in love with money if you are constantly giving it away. That makes no sense. Anyone making serious money and giving serious money away I would assert is in love not with money, but more than likely with Jesus. And that, my friends, is never a bad thing.

The other thing I love about Shooting Stars is they are passionate about helping other people with their health. The fact they get paid for helping families get more fruits, vegetables, berries, and plant-based omegas in their bodies is a benefit they need not feel guilty about. The reason I believe they are so successful as a team is because they are focused outwards, on others, not themselves. God rewards those who don't make life about themselves. I think too many times we as human beings want to make life about ourselves. We want to be the point because it makes us feel good inside. But guess what? We are not the point. Life has to be about others, that is the key to true success and happiness!

Diversity is always a key aspect to any organization that knows how to leverage it. The Shooting Stars are no exception. Each partner recruits people into the business who they want to work with, which is an appealing concept in it of itself. Being able to offer a home-based business to anyone who wants the opportunity to earn whatever they put into the business is both powerful and noble. People in this tribe come from all walks of life. Some are doctors, nurses, lawyers, bankers, managers, Olympic athletes, and other professional occupations. Still others are entrepreneurs, teachers, government workers, stay-at-home moms, retirees, personal trainers, hair stylists, yoga instructors, and military folks. Some have PhDs and some are high school dropouts. Some are men, some are women. Do you get the picture? They stem from all walks of life, from all races, and from various nationalities and ethnicities.

There is so much knowledge, wisdom, and strength in this diversity. If I have a question about something, anything, inevitably someone in the tribe has the answer. All we need to do is tap into it. If they don't know the answer, they know someone who does, so they point me in their direction. I enjoy connecting people to one another. If someone has a need for a babysitter for example, I can point them toward my friend Rachael's teenage daughter. Or if someone has a need for automotive services or repairs, I can connect them with my friend, Mark, who owns two auto service shops in town. Or perhaps someone needs a handyman, a plumber, an A/C repairman, a realtor, an attorney, a doctor, a nurse, a fitness expert, a security expert, or an HR specialist ... yep, I can point them in the right direction. There are many good reasons to find a like-minded tribe to do life with. More on that later. Do you have a tribe like this?

Every tribe needs a good place to hang out. For us in Cibolo, it became the 1908 House of Wine and Ale over on Main Street, owned by my dear friend, Lis Mathis. Her and her husband, Jayme, had a dream to take an old Victorian house and turn it into a wine bar and that's exactly what they did. Together with my son, Jesse, we took out the kitchen cabinets and sink before the real renovations started. Then my wife and I and several other members of the tribe helped sand and stain the tops of wooden spools you see in the bar today being used as tables. I guess you could say I have sweat equity in the place! But this is where countless conversations about how to build the Kingdom have been had. This is where we discuss our biggest dreams and desires. This is where we held packet pick-up for the 5K fundraisers we organized. This is where we celebrated my completing the Colson Fellows program. This is where we held one of Rachael's surprise birthday parties, and celebrated the birthdays of many others as well. This is where countless other tribal celebrations have taken place! It's simply one of the main local spots where we like to spend time with one another.

This is the tribe I have found. While the U.S. military is often labeled as the top one percent of the country, I would be so brave as to say Shooting Stars are the top one percent of the rest of the country. I have seen it with my own eyes. I have witnessed countless of them help, serve, and minister to others in need and in big ways. For example, I once witnessed my friend, Kristan, place socks on a homeless man's feet in the dead of winter. He was wearing only a tank top, shorts, and sandals. Kristan and I had brought some donations we had collected together with Danette, and when she saw this man so exposed to the cold weather she jumped into action and dressed him in multiple long-sleeve shirts, pants and even took off her own scarf (a very nice one at that) and placed it around his neck. After we prayed with him, the man was in tears, he could not believe the kindness shown to him that evening. Something this tribe does so naturally.

When my wife lost her mother, I can't overstate the level of generosity and compassion this tribe displayed. They showered her with flowers, gifts, and cards, they brought over food, and they even took us out for dinner. They sent text messages full of love, faith, and encouragement. They called me to ask how my wife was holding up and to see if it was ok to call her. It was such an awesome display of humanity. But this is just the way they are because they believe in Jesus and yearn to emulate Him knowing they will always fall short.

Losing a loved one is always difficult. Yet this tribe allows one another to help in grieving. They come together tightly when there is a death in one's family. My dear friend Katie lost her sixteen-year-old son to illness and disease a few years ago. My dear friend Kristan lost her mom a few years ago. My dear friend Danette lost her mom and then immediately also lost a dear cousin just a few years ago. My dear friend Lauren lost her husband a few years ago. My dear friend Rachael lost her grandmother last year. And as I mentioned, my wife lost her mother last year. I say all of this to let you know that despite the loss of dear loved ones, the tribe remains focused on doing all they can for God, all this goodness for Jesus. Because they know they have the love and support of the tribe to get them through those hard times when we yearn for those who have passed away. We lift each other up and love each other deeply.

Why do I belabor these points? Because as a man dealing with internal demons related to my past, this tribe took me in and gave me back the ability to dream again. To overcome mental health challenges. They reinstilled my faith in humanity. While the power of a single individual can be huge, the power of a tribe can be epic! It was in meeting these human beings I realized I no longer hated people. So, if you are battling PTSD, get yourself a tribe like mine, or just join mine!

10

TRIAD OF TRANSFORMATION

> *"Do not be conformed to this world, but be transformed by the renewal of your mind, that by testing you may discern what is the will of God, what is good and acceptable and perfect." – Romans 12:2*

BEING in a tribe like the Shooting Stars means you are going to grow and develop as a person, whether you realize it or not. As I began to seriously heal from the impact of PTSD, I began to study why I was able to do so without seeing any doctors or taking any medications. I came to the conclusion there were three things that contributed to my being able to manage my PTSD and become "high-functioning." Those three things were whole-food nutrition and movement (diet and exercise), a solid village or tribe (community), and spirituality (faith).

First let's talk about whole-food nutrition. A dear friend of mine, Ms. Jennifer Myers, sent me a book, titled *The Transformation: Discovering Wholeness and Healing After Trauma*, by James S. Gordon, MD. Although I never physically saw a doctor for my PTSD, I did heed the advice in this book. It helped me understand what was happening to me!

Please bear with me as I nerd out on the science for a bit. You see, according to Dr. Gordon, when we are stressed, signals from the hypothalamus reach the pituitary gland, which in turn tells the outer part, or cortex, of our adrenal glands to secrete cortisol and other stress hormones. Cortisol helps us retain water, raises our blood pressure, and mobilizes sugar from our cells, activating and nourishing us and stimulating our mental functioning.

The problem is that high levels of cortisol destroy cells in the hippocampus. This is not good because this is the part of the brain that controls your memory and regulates stress. It has the ability to lessen our immune response. Over time, people who are traumatized are unable to appropriately respond to stress because their adrenal gland seems "exhausted."

Oh, and by the way, the traumatic event that caused your neurotransmitter dopamine to initially spike, well it now declines along with your levels of serotonin. While dopamine provides that energy (and it just feels good), serotonin does the opposite. It calms you down. So if your serotonin tanks, we may slip into depression. This is one of the reasons I, struggling with PTSD, felt chronically tired all the time.

The changes caused in the brain by PTSD can last a very long time. According to Dr. Gordon, they can last for the duration of a war, an abusive relationship, or while coping with an ominous medical diagnosis and its painful treatment. And get this, these responses can persist even when the actual trauma is long over!

Dr. Gordon said something in his book that just rattled me. He said our brain may replay traumatic memories over and over again, and these memories can affect us just as profoundly as the original trauma and can significantly prolong and even compound the physical and emotional damage. We may find ourselves chained to our past, repeating the stress or trauma forever. This biological and psychological damage can then lead to heart disease, diabetes, immune disorders, cancer, and alcoholism. Can any of you relate?

Also, did you know that not keeping your microbiome (lining in the gut) healthy can impact our brain health? I had no idea, and this is the reason I drink kombucha. The good bacteria that lives in our small intestine decreases when we are stressed, spiking the bad bacteria. So, as you can imagine, processed foods (fast-foods), artificial sugars, and genetically modified foods all negatively impact our health, and if we're trying to recover from PTSD, the impact to our brain health is so detrimental! To counter all of these negative effects, we need whole-food nutrition. A high intake of fruits, vegetables, and berries have all the nutrients your body needs to begin to heal itself. Your body knows what to do with natural wholefoods!

Remember when I told you I was dealing with high blood pressure, high cholesterol, and diabetes? Natural wholefoods and the plant powders found in Juice Plus (and a few other simple changes) are how I began to come off all prescription medications for these things. I also dropped about forty pounds in the process! My energy was back and so was my ability to obtain and maintain an erection! I know, TMI, but you can imagine my wife's elation when she realized I could make love to her again. Heck, I can't tell you how good I felt, like a man on a mountain, ready to take on the world! Some of you know exactly what I am talking about because you too have experienced this!

The second part of the triad is being part of a community, a village, a tribe. Since the beginning, God's plan calls for us to be in community with one another. As I said earlier, my tribe gets it and has meaningful relationships with one another. The Shooting Stars serve, encourage, share, and faithfully chase Jesus! They have provided a safe place for me and everyone else where we celebrate accomplishments and achievements along with those setbacks or dark moments in our lives. This tribe shows up consistently in my life both for the magnificent and the mundane. They know God and absolutely want to be the best versions of themselves to better serve Him, all while helping others do the same. Remember when I said you are not the point. My tribe knows how to make life about others. This is what they do best!

In this life, we are better together. There is no other way to flourish biblically. As I write this, COVID-19 and its variants have caused many people to isolate themselves in their homes. Perhaps this is one of you reading this book? Living in solitude is exactly what the enemy wants. Don't give him what he wants! He knows how to employ tried and true military tactics against us, such as cutting off communications to isolate us and then probing our defenses. 1 Peter 5:8 tells us to, "Be sober-minded; be watchful. Your adversary the devil prowls around like a roaring lion, seeking someone to devour." The devil knows our hearts yearn for godly relationships and the richness those relationships can bring to ourselves and others. If you are isolating, this is why you feel that void in your life, in your heart, for fellowship with others.

One of our tribe's most favorite way of getting together is called Hymns and Hops. It is an event put on by a local brewery

REDEMPTION OF A COUNTERSPY

in the town of New Braunfels called Five Stones Brewery, owned by a local guy named Seth. My friend Danette likes to describe Seth as a "modern day monk." He loves him some Jesus. And so, every six weeks or so he hosts Hymns and Hops at the brewery that includes a live performance by a Christian band that plays classic hymns with a modern sound, and of course, beer. Hey, don't judge me, Christians! We don't get drunk at the event, and all the proceeds from that night go to a local charity, a different one chosen by Seth each time, isn't that cool?! We grab a hymn book and sing along with the band in an outdoor space in front of the brewery. It is like a small park with lots of trees for shade. We show up with lawn chairs and sometimes even food to share with each other. Those with kids can let them run around and just be kids. The little ones play in the dirt, play tag, and climb on rock piles while the older ones throw a football or a Frisbee around or just sit in circles on the ground discussing the latest high school adventures. It is a great way to be in each other's company, with our families, singing our hearts out to Jesus!

Being a member of my tribe reminds me of Acts 2 of the Bible. It describes an entire tribe of like-minded people who spent their days breaking bread together, laughing with one another, praying together, and just having a good time together. They unleashed generosity, as my pastor likes to frame it, toward anyone in need. These people constantly welcomed newcomers to the faith and made it a point to pour into one another consistently. My tribe is just like them. My tribe are a bunch of Jesus loving Christians. We are found people who find people!

Here are some examples of what I am talking about. My tribe:

- Donates money to help a friend in an unexpected financial crisis.
- Attends sporting events of each other's kids.
- Works out together.
- Celebrates each other's birthdays . . . sometime for the entire month.
- Travels together to conferences, retreats, summits, or even just together on vacation.
- Encourages each other when someone is having a bad day.
- Gives gifts; my tribe does this for just about any occasion and sometimes just because!
- Shows up at the hospital when a friend has an emergency.
- Gets together to celebrate holidays.
- Goes out to dinner together.
- And sometimes, they do nothing more than offer a much-needed hug to one another.

Even when relationships get messy (because that does happen sometimes), my tribe endures the difficulty and challenges because godly relationships are worth it. In my Juice Plus tribe, we believe we must always be our authentic selves with everyone we meet. This is important. If you are reading this and struggling with PTSD, you should know it is ok to get angry, sad, frustrated, or overwhelmed with life's challenges. The key is not staying in that space for too long. If there is one thing I have learned in this journey of life, it is that just like every other feeling, happiness really is a choice. I can choose to be upset for a little while before making the choice to be happy again. Master that, and you can live your best life always.

Positivity is important, but it can't be consistent. Read that again. If you have nothing but positivity despite circumstances, then you are not being authentic. And it is not healthy for you or your tribe. It is toxic positivity. When things go wrong, or there are contentious issues, or you get bad news, or you are disappointed by your tribe, being authentic means you should get angry, upset, sad, heartbroken, etc. It does not give you permission to disrespect anyone, but it is ok to let others know you are not happy, or you have a concern. That is real. That is raw. That is authentic. In those moments, nobody likes to hear someone glossing over the issue and proclaiming how good life is no matter what. That is most definitely not authentic. It comes from a good place, even a loving heart, but it is misguided and does nothing more than disrespect and demean the feelings of others who may be having an emotional moment. Just acknowledge the problem and give people a safe place to vent their frustration, and then provide hope and direction. This is leadership 101. But I digress!

The third member of the triad is spirituality. After coming off all prescription medications, dropping almost forty pounds in eight months, and changing up my diet with one simple change at a time, I was now armed with new information to help both my physical and mental health. And with Rachael helping me to improve my spiritual health, I felt confident I could really turn things around and become the best version of myself possible. My pastor, Pastor Zak White of my newfound church, Revolution Church, handed out some affirmations like the ones I previously provided you in Part I of this book. Affirmations are important, and they really do work to sort of re-program the mind. You have to be careful what you speak to yourself, because your brain will go out and try to make that your reality, to prove you right!

Here are the affirmations from Pastor Zak, use them daily during your quiet time:

1. I walk in divine health. – Isaiah 53:5
2. I live under an open heaven. – Malachi 3:10
3. I have no lack for any good thing. – Psalms 23:1
4. I expect favor with God and with man. – Luke 2:52
5. I live in abundance. – John 10:10
6. My God shall supply all of my needs according to His riches and glory in Christ. – Philippians 4:19
7. I walk in the fruit of the Spirit. – Galatians 5:22-23
8. I hear from God. – John 10:27
9. My steps are ordered by the Lord. – Proverbs 16:9
10. God is my strength, and I can do all things through Christ who strengthens me. – Philippians 4:13
11. I walk by faith and not by sight. – 2 Corinthians 5:7
12. I enjoy my work and make the most of my time. – Colossians 3:23
13. I have supernatural wisdom and discernment. – James 1:5
14. I walk in revelation knowledge. – Matthew 16:17
15. The gifts of the Spirit operate in my life. – 1 Corinthians 12:4
16. I live every day in abundant joy. – Romans 15:13
17. I will fulfill my calling and the destiny that God has for me. – Ephesians 2:10
18. I expect God's best. – Luke 11:11-13
19. I use my talents and gifts to glorify God. – 1 Peter

4:10-11
20. I have the mind of Christ. – 1 Corinthians 2:16
21. I have a teachable spirit. – Psalms 32:8
22. I receive what I ask for, I find what I'm looking for, and the doors are open in my life. – Matthew 7:7

Spirituality, for me, is what turned it all around for permanent good. It gave me a sense of peace and balanced the various aspects of my life whether they be physical, mental, or spiritual. Various spiritual communities encourage one to join up with like-minded people in spiritual worship, such as church attendance. Going to church is important because, again, we're not meant to do life alone. Attending church regularly allows us to be encouraged by our congregation and the relationships we form there, to be enlightened by the word as explained by a pastor, and to serve others through the different venues a church might provide. These things provide a sense of belonging. They can also become the tribe you need to overcome challenges with PTSD, depression or suicidal ideation. I once read an article that talked about how strong relationships have proven to increase general wellbeing and even, get this, bolster life expectancy! The article also talked about a study that found a strong association between church attendance and improved health, mood, and wellbeing.

Spiritual people have a way of finding ways to "-meet the challenge and continue with purposeful lives . . . they bounce back and carry on." That's a quote from Dr. Steven Southwick's book, *Resilience: The Science of Mastering Life's Greatest Challenges*.

Don't get me wrong, after I was saved it wasn't like I lived happily ever after, but I have lived peacefully ever since. There are still struggles in my life, but spirituality helps me find meaning in my day-to-day struggles, in my painful experiences. It also helps me realize and understand that disappointment is just part of our human experience on this earth, and that I am not alone in my struggles.

People often say to me, "Sammy, how do you sleep at night with everything you've been through and everything you've seen?" Well, I put it to them like this:

The human experience is marked by contrast. The comforts of peace and prosperity are witnessed together next to the tragedy of war and poverty. I believe our Creator uses both to teach us life is both precious and painful. Think about the joy we experience during the birth of a child. Are you imagining what that feels like? The immense happiness and love. Now think about the pain you feel when you lose someone you love. It is difficult, isn't it? So then, let me ask you, how would we recognize joy if there was no pain? How would we come to appreciate light if there was no darkness? How could we possibly know what love is, without hate? How would we come to appreciate life if there was no death? It is just profound. Contemplating these thoughts can give one clarity of purpose. And in my humble opinion, the purpose of life is to spread the good news. This in turn can serve to alleviate pain and suffering, to share hope, to feed the hungry, and to find truth.

If you're battling PTSD, depression, or suicidal ideations, please allow me to summarize all of this for you. My Triad of Transformation concept includes wholefood nutrition and getting up and moving. That's how you start to counter the effects that stress, trauma, anxiety, and depression have had on your body. For me, it was the plant powders or micronutrients found in Juice Plus that helped, but whatever you choose, make sure it makes it easy for you to flood your body with the full gambit of nutrition from a variety of fruits, vegetables, and berries that also have an NSF certification, that way you can be confident what they say is in their product is actually the truth.

Find yourself a tribe of like-minded people to do life with. After all, we are not meant to do life alone and are much better together. Let them love you unconditionally, let them pour into you and encourage you always! Together with your tribe, nothing is impossible, and you can embark on your own mission to start a revolution of grace in one life at a time!

And finally, do yourself a favor and dive into some form of spirituality. This is what brings the Triad of Transformation together, it is the glue that binds it all up together for good. For me, it was Jesus who set me on a path that brought me right here, right now, in this moment, as your "hope dealer." I am a found person who finds people, I am a changed person who changes people, and if I am, you can be too.

PART FOUR

SAVED PEOPLE WHO SERVE PEOPLE

11

MY DIRTY TOWEL

> *"Jesus, knowing that the Father had given all things into his hands, and that he had come from God and was going back to God, rose from supper. He laid aside his outer garments, and taking a towel, tied it around his waist. Then he poured water into a basin and began to wash the disciples' feet and to wipe them with the towel that was wrapped around him." — John 13:3-5*

I DO NOT KNOW who said it or who posted it, but I once read a meme on social media that said, "Sometimes I joke about what I'd do if I had one day left to live. Eat junk, go crazy, etc. Today it hit me: Jesus knew. And he washed feet."

One of my favorite lessons I learned upon returning to Christ is found in John, chapter 13 of the Holy Bible, verses 3-5. In them, Jesus, the one who walks on water, who calms the storm, who heals, who raises the dead, the one who is basically the most wonderful being in existence, is down on his knees in front of twelve men. He has a basin and a towel and begins washing their feet in an ultimate display of humility. Men wore sandals in those days, and so you can imagine how dirty those twenty-four feet must have been. Also, washing feet was slave work! Kings certainly did not wash feet, but here was the King of Kings on his knees doing just that. Through His actions, He tells us we should serve others. That we should be humble, and even though He knew one of those men would betray Him, He washed that man's feet anyway. He tells us to face those things that disgust and repel us, and instead of turning away from them, we should run toward them. What if you could be a blessing to the ones who repel you the most? He sets the example for us all by washing the dirty, stinky, filthy feet of those twelve men.

Tricia and I once met a couple who seemed to be good friends to us, but we later learned the wife had said some less than kind things about Tricia behind her back and had a bad habit of attempting to manipulate other women for her own agenda. So of course we stopped hanging out with them. The women's husband, as it turned out, was a womanizer and once spoke disrespectfully about my friend and spiritual mentor, Rachael. Needless to say Tricia and I wanted nothing to do with these two, so we kept our distance, we were repelled by them. I even told my wife that they offered nothing we needed or wanted in a relationship, so we cut them off. But later my wife decided she would be the bigger person and forgave the woman for her comments and treated her cordially. Tricia stopped avoiding her and instead sought to cease the drama between them. Following my wife's lead, I ended up doing the same with the woman's husband.

Jesus calls on all of us to go from consumers to contributors. Consumers seek to receive, they move toward whatever is for them, and they continue to return to that which gives. It is ok to have a consumer inside you, but at some point Jesus is hoping you go from 'what can I get,' to 'what can I give?' This is the paradigm shift Jesus wants from us! He wants us to be the generous ones, the loving ones who give before we receive, who give without even expecting to receive! Having been saved, I was now ready to be a serious contributor!

The spirit of God gave everyone a gift, a talent . . . even me! He expects me to use it to benefit others, not myself! You are called to do the same, we all are! And it does not mean your contribution has to be grand. As the saying goes, it is the little things in life that matter. A life well lived is when you can say, "I served to the best of my ability, the best I could, and the more I blessed other people, the more God blessed my life!" This is what I personally believe God is looking for in all of us. What does it look like to wash each other's feet? To get your towel dirty? Jesus desires a church where people serve more than they have been served. The Son of Man came to serve, not to be served! And what an example He set for us to follow!

I believe I have always had a servant's heart in my nature, but once I understood this about God, I took it to a whole new level. I began by serving with my church on Sundays, but that was not enough. I needed to really get my towel dirty. Because I could relate to those struggling with PTSD, I decided to use my experiences to help others afflicted in the same manner. I decided to take a negative and turn it into a positive. Since I have been told

I have a way with words, I capitalized on that talent and began speaking publicly about PTSD in order to raise public awareness and possibly provide hope where perhaps hope has been lost. I found it very therapeutic to recount my story out loud. There is a healing that happens within when we verbalize our pain to others. When I first announced I was struggling with PTSD, it was as if a heavy weight had been lifted from my shoulders. And vulnerability breeds vulnerability.

Public speaking gigs were still not enough, I felt God calling me to do more. So I decided to organize a family 5K fun run to raise money for Project Healing Heroes doing business as CombatPTSD.org, a non-profit organization dedicated to helping combat veterans and first responders (as well as their spouses) battle the invisible wounds of war and trauma. Dr. David Tharp, the organization's founder, wrote a manual designed to leverage the training veterans learned in the military, and use it to battle and overcome their challenges with PTSD. I found the manual very effective in my own fight against my demons. So with the help of my wife, Rachael, and a few other servants from my tribe, like Debbye, Gina, Dido, and Danette to name a few, we raised just over 10K for CombatPTSD.org the first year! It increased every year following that for the next four years!

But I was now addicted to getting my towel dirty, and because of the fundraiser, I was now a known member of the community for helping veterans, so out from the woodwork they came. One by one I began helping veterans with their struggle against depression and suicide. Old military buddies and strangers alike began reaching out to me and telling me about the demons they were facing. Often times we would pray over the phone, some of these men were on the brink of suicide and had to be "talked off the ledge" so to speak. Others needed professional help, so I arranged to have them admitted to Camp Hope, a facility and program belonging to the PTSD Foundation, another non-profit organization dedicated to the fight against PTSD. Veterans can stay there for up to six months at no cost to them as they receive counseling and other relevant services to help them manage their PTSD. It is amazing to watch these men transform their lives in a positive way!

And they weren't just veterans who came to me, and not just adults either, teenagers began to call me. One of them was the sixteen-year-old son of a very close friend of mine. I'll never forget the night he called me. It was around 11 pm when I answered my phone.

"Hello?" I said, realizing it was him through the caller ID.

"Hey Sam, it's me, (name omitted)." He sounded tired.

"Hey, what's going on?" I asked him.

"Oh nothing, I'm sorry for calling so late, but I just need to talk to someone," he explained.

"Of course, no worries, man, tell me what's going on," I said to him.

"I don't know . . . I just feel like, well . . . uhm, I just . . . sometimes I feel like I just want to drive my car over a bridge. I'm just not sure I want to live anymore," he said.

I was in shock. This was a kid I have known since he was about five years old, and I knew his parents well. I was thankful he trusted me enough to call me, because he had not told his dad about what he was feeling. We ended up talking until after midnight, and I followed up with him for the next several weeks. I also ended up telling his dad, because God forbid the kid do something and his mom and dad find out I knew he was struggling.

His dad was very appreciative for the call and said he knew something was going on with his son. In the end, we helped his son overcome his demons and he is alive today.

Let me make one thing perfectly clear, all of this is God's doing . . . ALL OF IT. I give all praise and glory to Him, and I am thankful He began working through me as I overcame my demons and the whispers of the enemy, as I began to heal from my invisible wounds. I understand I can take no credit for any of this, so all glory to Him.

Often times when Veterans separate or retire from service, they lose that common sense of camaraderie. These are people who are used to getting their towel dirty, the military way of life is grounded in teamwork, in serving others before yourself. You quickly learn you are an integral part of a bigger team, and if you fail in your individual duties and responsibilities, the entire team and subsequently the entire mission fails. This is why you learn to help each other out early in the process of transforming from a civilian to a military man or woman, because nobody wants the mission to fail. And nobody wants to be the reason the mission fails either!

The same is true in sports; however, in the military, mission failure means people die. Individuals who may have joined the military to serve their country quickly realize it is all about the man next to them in combat. Nobody is thinking about their country in a firefight, they are thinking of their fellow warriors who are fighting right next to them. If you are a combat Veteran reading this, you know exactly what I mean. You would much rather die than leave your brother warriors behind. They become the only reason your towel is dirty, and in the culture of the world's greatest military, the dirtier the better.

Veterans also sometimes lose their sense of purpose when they leave the military. You veterans know what I am talking about. When you were in the military, you had immense responsibilities. You worked on helicopters, you drove tanks, you were on a crew served weapon team, you rigged parachutes, you drove armored personnel carriers and worked on HMMWVs. You had a purpose, and your team needed you. All of that is instantly gone when you get out. You find yourself lost in a sea of civilians. Sometimes you struggle to hold down a job, or cannot work at all due to your medical history related to the military and/or your PTSD. Caretakers end up with two jobs or more, causing stress and tension in the home and in the relationships. It becomes a struggle just to put food on the table and keep shelter overhead. And these are people who sacrificed so much, put it all on the line for an often ungrateful nation. For me, I found my peace in serving.

And yet, to me it seemed my towel was never dirty enough. So I volunteered to serve on the City of Cibolo's Historic Committee in an effort to make a difference in my small town. I realized in my studies of Jesus that He could bring peace and grace to anyone if they simply sought His love. So I set out to be His disciple and missionary by sharing Jesus. The city was no exception, sometimes people just need someone to listen to them, a simple hug or any simple act of kindness or gesture that lets them know they are not alone, that someone actually cares. I also found that bringing people to Jesus means you have to go out into the world and meet more people! You cannot retreat into the confines of your comfort zone and let life happen to you, you must go out and make a noble life while getting your towel as filthy as possible!

Well, an opportunity to get my towel absolutely soiled came when I was asked by my church to help bring our church service to the male inmates at the Briscoe Unit, a Texas state penitentiary. Now, that did not sound appealing to me at all. The prison is over an hour away, I have never been to prison, and the ministry would take place on a Tuesday night, a work night, where I would come home late in the evening having to wake up early the next morning for work. I just wasn't interested.

However, God had other plans, and I simply needed to be obedient. As I prayed on it, I felt the Holy Spirit was tugging at me, guiding me to go and save as many souls as possible within that prison! It became one of my favorite ways to serve, going before 160+ men doing time behind bars and sharing the gospel and the love of Jesus Christ with them.

Within a few years of being saved, I was an advocate for Juice Plus, a fundraiser, sat on the Board for Project Healing Heroes, served on the Cibolo Historic Committee, was a member of God Behind Bars with my church, and was the Director of Safety at my church. Oh, and by the way, I still had my government day job as well as the job of a husband, father, and grandfather! Needless to say, my towel needed a good wash. But I didn't have time to wash it, I kept getting it dirtier and dirtier.

That's when one of the members of my tribe, Shane Moon, approached me with an idea for a non-profit. He was interested in launching Strategic Global Commissioning, Inc., a 501(c)3 non-profit dedicated to providing threat information and mitigation measures for Christian missionaries taking the Gospel out into foreign lands. The services are designed to keep missionaries safe as they spread the Gospel, and they are provided at zero cost to them or their sending organizations. Shane wanted my help launching this company, and how could I say no to that very noble cause?! I jumped at the chance and over the last three years as of the writing of this book have grown the company to be an invaluable resource for missionaries.

I was serving in many capacities. Something else I learned in my journey back to Christ is the difference between volunteers and servants. You may very well know many from each category, although you may never have thought about them in this perspective. In my humble opinion, volunteers are those people who sort of check the box in terms of their service. They mean well, they just don't have the passion behind their service. Their motives are not necessarily malicious but can often times be selfish or self-serving. What I mean by that is often times volunteers sign up for things because of outside pressure, perhaps from a family member, friend, or an organization such as a church or school, and they want to satisfy that external pressure. Sometimes they may do it to gain status within a church or other organization and be seen as the types who always help out. Once their volunteer time is over, they consider it enough and go home. None of what I have described thus far is necessarily bad, the mere fact they have volunteered time and energy is a blessing in it of itself. Often the reason things get done is because of these very people. But if they are focused on themselves, on gaining favor with God and/or expecting some reciprocity, then they are missing the point completely.

A servant on the other hand can never be fulfilled in his or her service. They are making life about others, not themselves. Their hearts yearn for more, their efforts are never enough. Servants are not checking a box; they are fulfilling a deep desire to love their fellow human beings beyond status or impressing others. They are being obedient to Him and doing what Jesus Christ demanded of all of us, to love one another.

Have you served more than you have been served? What would this world be like if your mantra was one of, "How can I serve and bless everybody else?!" Remember what I said earlier, this life is not about you! Jesus desires a church where people give more than they receive. Jesus gave way more than he received, he gave his life for us! Jesus' number one message to the world, was love. Love one another. Jesus desires a church where people love more than they will ever be loved. He loved unconditionally, imagine if we could all do the same.

At my church we say, "I am deeply loved, highly favored, totally righteous, and destined to reign, all because of Jesus!" Run to people who repel you, run to those who are a mess. The only true legacy we leave behind when it is all said and done is not the biggest house, the fanciest car, the name brand clothes, or the expensive toys! No, it is the love we demonstrate to the children we raise, the people we mentor, the example we set for others to follow. And all of that combined will amount to one heck of a dirty towel. Therefore, I assert the one with the dirtiest towel wins . . . how dirty is your towel?

12

WORLDVIEW

> *"Preach the word; be ready in season and out of season; reprove, rebuke, and exhort, with complete patience and teaching. For the time is coming when people will not endure sound teaching, but having itching ears they will accumulate for themselves teachers to suit their own passions, and will turn away from listening to the truth and wander off into myths." – 2 Timothy 4:2-4*

BACK IN 2017, one of my goals entering the new year of 2018 was to learn more scripture and be able to recite it. You know those people who seem to always be able to quote you a verse from the bible in just about any conversation? Well, I decided I wanted to be more like them. It just so happened my friend Rachael invited me to go through a bible plan with her in the Uversion bible app. It was 365 days of daily devotionals that took us through the entire bible and allowed us to comment on what we learned to each other following each devotional. This kept me on track and engaged in scripture on a daily basis. Now, the reason I began diving into scripture was to be able to quote bible verses . . . not a good reason because remember how I said we should not make life about us? Well, trying to memorize bible verses just so I can quote them and thereby making me seem smart, brings the focus to myself; however, in a divine, super-natural way I began to hunger and thirst for more Jesus. I couldn't get enough and found myself speaking to God constantly each day, and not just once but multiple times throughout the day! I began thanking Him consistently for everything in my life and giving Him all the glory for anything going right in my life. The little things that would normally bother me began to no longer matter. I learned that when things are going right in your life is when you should speak more to Jesus, to give him praise and glory. My relationships at work improved, my relationship with my wife drastically improved as I strived to be more like the man she originally fell in love with, and by doing so I unconsciously reminded her WHY she once fell in love with me.

While I believe scripture is the number one way to grow closer to God, something else I did was develop a habit of literally speaking to God, not just in prayer and not just at night or in the morning, but throughout the day. I speak to God while in the car driving anywhere, I speak to Him when I first walk into my office at work and then throughout the workday, I speak to Him when I'm home, while in the shower, at a restaurant, at the carwash, even at my favorite wine bar. I laugh with Him and sometimes cry with

Him, but regardless of circumstances, it is always WITH Him. I consistently ask Him to come into my life, I acknowledge Him as my Lord and Savior out loud. Throughout the day I say to the Holy Spirit, "You are welcomed here," as I place my hand over my heart. Then I ask Him to please "teach, coach, and guide me" through the week.

When my wife and I began attending Revolution Church, I immediately fell in love with their worship team. One thing the lead singer said once that really resonated with me was that they are not there to entertain us; they are there to lead us in worship as we focus on the words of the songs and call Jesus into our hearts. I had never heard any worship team say that in any church. Following the time of worship, Pastor Zak, the lead pastor, not only talked us through scripture, but he immediately gave us practical ways to implement that scripture in our lives using a host of analogies, some of them funny, some not so much, but all equally important. I really bought into his use of props to illustrate biblical concepts, as well as the church's use of technology, such as the Rev Church App, their website, quick and easy online forms for registering for various events, and even his use of movie clips to facilitate teaching points. Today, anyone can catch the live stream at Revyourlife.com. Like Everyday Christian Fellowship, Revolution Church is also housed in a warehouse converted into a church. Pastor Zak and his wife Amber are some of the most down-to-earth yet hip leaders of a church I have ever met.

At Revolution Church, Pastor Zak taught me how the church is like a hospital, full of sick people. Church is not for perfect people; we are all sinners. It's for the sick, who once are healed, go out and heal other sick people! He often says that Christians need to become comfortable, being uncomfortable. This is such good advice for life! Because we don't grow as human beings, in the comfort zone. We have to step out of that comfortable space in order to be used mightily as an instrument of God's will and design! Another thing Pastor Zak always says is we have to keep our "-mind on the mission and the mission on our mind!" Come on now, you gotta love that!

Being a Christian does not mean I am perfect and without sin. As far as I am concerned, there is only one perfect person who ever walked this earth, and his name is Jesus. You can't just be good and get to Heaven. Because good people do not go to Heaven, forgiven people do. You can't earn your way into Heaven, Jesus died to make a way for us to enter His Kingdom if only we repent of our sins, ask Him for forgiveness, and believe Jesus died for our sins and was resurrected three days later. Invite Him into your heart, into your life, into a relationship with you. This is the only way to get to Heaven.

As you can see, my faith was growing, my faith journey was on the move. It was then my friend James George sent me an email encouraging me to sign up for a program called the Colson Fellows. It is an intense, ten month study in Christian worldview. Students read approximately thirteen books during the program and read daily devotionals followed by answering deep questions about what they read in an online student portal. There are also live webinars students must attend, where various authors, biblical scholars, ministers, and other academics lecture on a specific Christian worldview topic. Students also read articles from the internet and watch videos from the Bible Project online, then answer questions as well as discuss the material in the online portal. Monthly cohort meetings are also held to discuss the readings from the books and ensure students are progressing satisfactorily through the program. Toward the end of the ten months, students must pick something they have learned in the program and teach it to an audience of their choice. It is true what they say about those who learn, then they teach. The capstone project is the final task in order to satisfy commissioning requirements (you don't technically graduate from the program; you earn a commission). It calls for students to develop a three-year strategic plan for a ministry of their choice, which they will execute following commissioning. This is why they say you are commissioned, because they commission you to step out in faith in this fallen world in order to purposefully expand the Kingdom of God.

As I finished reading James' email and the Colson Fellows' program description, I was very much intrigued. I went to the program website to learn more, as I had never heard of this program. Turns out it was first established by the Colson Center as the Centurions Program. The Colson Center was founded by Chuck Colson, an attorney during the Nixon administration who was caught up in the Watergate Scandal. He served some time in prison, where he found Jesus and started up Prison Fellowship, the largest prison ministry in the nation. In 1991, he founded the Colson Center. This excerpt is taken right from the Colson Fellows website:

"Chuck Colson, the founder of the Colson Fellows Program, understood personally that God has the power to accomplish great things through imperfect people. His own trials and the redemption he found in Jesus Christ inspired Chuck to build a robust discipleship program that would reverse the Christian evacuation from intellectual life and the public square. Today, this program equips Colson Fellows from all walks of life with a biblical

imagination that enables them to understand the times and respond faithfully in any arena God has called them to."

Following Chuck's death in 2012, the Centurions were renamed Colson Fellows, in his honor.

I sent the link to my wife and to Rachael, asking them what they thought. Rachael replied with, "Sounds amazing!" While my wife replied with, "Don't you think you already have enough on your plate?!" I had to laugh! She was right! The program called for a modest investment in money and a significant investment in time. Time is something I am able to manage only with the help of Google Calendar. I did have a lot on my plate but this, this was a whole other level of seeking Jesus! So, I prayed on it for a day. I say a day because God answered me so strongly, I was immediately convinced of my decision to enroll. The program was starting within a week from the time I received James' email. I filled out the application, answering all the questions as best I could. Most questions centered on my faith and my faith journey . . . so I had a lot to say! I got everything turned in and was accepted just a couple of days prior to day one of the program.

One of the reasons I decided to apply for this program (besides the fact I felt I was being obedient) was because I felt it would bring me closer to Jesus. I thought the daily devotionals alone would keep my focus on Him, and they did. Coupled with the daily readings in the books (which were absolutely phenomenal by the way), I felt my level of understanding of God begin to rise and rise quickly. I forced myself to slow down and absorb the lessons. Here is my reading list of the books from the program, in case you're interested.

1. Colson, Charles W.; Pearcey, Nancy. *How Now Shall We Live?*

2. Packer, J.I. *Knowing God.*
3. Lewis, C.S. *Mere Christianity.*
4. Phillips, W. Gary; Brown, William E; Stonestreet, John. *Making Sense of the World: A Biblical Worldview.*
5. Sunshine, Glenn. *Why You Think the Way You Do.*
6. Gould, Paul. *Cultural Apologetics: Renewing the Christian Voice, Conscience, and Imagination in a Disenchanted World.*
7. Koukl, Greg. *Tactics: A Game Plan for Discussing Your Christian Conviction.*
8. Stonestreet, John; Kunkle, Brett. *A Practical Guide to Culture: Helping the Next Generation Navigate Today's World.*
9. Qureshi, Nabeel. *Seeking Allah, Finding Jesus: A Devout Muslim Encounters Christianity.*
10. Guinness, Os. *Carpe Diem Redeemed: Seizing the Day, Discerning the Times.*
11. Yuan, Christopher. *Holy Sexuality and the Gospel: Sex, Desire, and Relationships Shaped by God's Grand Story.*
12. Sherman, Amy. *Kingdom Calling: Vocational Stewardship for the Common Good.*
13. Stonestreet, John; Smith, Warren Cole. *Restoring All Things: God's Audacious Plan to Change the World through Everyday People.*

Most of these books are available on Amazon. They are placed in the order in which they were required to be read by the Colson Fellows program. Have you read any of these books?

I believe I told one of my friends that most of the questions I ever had about God were answered in the book by J.I. Packer, *Knowing God.*

Through this program I learned about culture. Do you realize every song you listen to and movie you watch is encouraging you to believe and act a certain way? Even the internet, video games, television, and basically the entire entertainment industry with all its technology is communicating values and ideas to everyone. Do you recognize the worldview messages found in the culture surrounding you and your family? How much of an impact is it making on your values and behavior? It really is powerful and will influence how you and your kids dress, talk, and perceive other human beings. It is so important to ensure you watch television or listen to music through a critically biblical lens. We must evaluate everything and discern the world around us. The influence culture has on us is strong, and it happens very subtly. The Colson Fellows program gave me the knowledge and skills to discern the culture and recognize the various worldviews inherent to every song, movie, and television show I am exposed to.

As Christians, this is especially important for our teenagers. You want them to think deeply about life and this fallen world around them. We do not want them to be molded or conditioned to think a certain way by pop-culture. We want them to learn to be critical thinkers who, in the process of discerning and evaluating life, find truth.

When your teens go off into the world, whether it be college, the military, or even the workforce, you want them to know in their heart of hearts that Christianity, and ONLY Christianity, can answer ALL of life's ultimate questions with answers that stand the test of time. The question of origins: From where did everything come from? The question of meaning: Why are we here? The question of morality: How are we to live? And the question of destiny: What happens after we die?

While other religions and belief systems may have answers to

REDEMPTION OF A COUNTERSPY

some of these questions, they don't withstand hard scrutiny. We cannot pretend these questions do not exist or believe it is possible to ignore them. They come up in in times of tragedy, in decisions about our future, or when someone says something that contradicts our world view. These questions have been around since history started being recorded. How we answer them depends on our worldview, and Christians should always strive to sharpen the lens by which they view the world in order to ensure we are living biblical lives.

My PTSD caused me to have a very warped worldview. As I described earlier, I was having dark thoughts about people in general. The enemy was using my PTSD to slowly pry me away from any beliefs in God. You see, a worldview is your interpretation of the world, and that interpretation determines how you live your life, how you behave. In the Colson Fellows program, we were taught that your worldview is more than your view OF the world, it is your view FOR the world. People do not always live what they profess, but they will live what they believe. Read that again. It is simply unavoidable.

There are generally three major worldviews. One could argue there are more, but all of them will generally fall into one of these three: Naturalism, Transcendentalism, and Theism. I will summarize each one for you very quickly.

Naturalism is the belief that everything formed naturally in our universe because there is no God. You and I are accidents; everything is physical, not metaphysical.

Transcendentalism is the belief that God does not exist as we Christians believe Him to exist. That is, as a personal being we can be in relation with through Jesus Christ. Transcendentalism believes God is an impersonal, spiritual, or psychic force that those with the right knowledge can leverage for their own use. Many Eastern religions fall into this category.

Then there is Theism, a belief in one God who is an entity or a being with whom we can talk to through prayer and through His word found in holy texts. Jews, Muslims, and Christians all subscribe to Theism. While all three believe a single God created the universe, Christians are set apart from the other two by our belief in the fact Jesus Christ is the Son of God and made a way for us to have a deep personal relationship with God.

If you call yourself Christian, is there anything in your home that depicts a different worldview? What are you going to do about it? Each worldview I described determines how you answer the ultimate questions of life and influences how you conduct yourself. Do you conduct yourself in a manner befitting a Christian worldview? This is everything I pondered as I went through the Colson Fellows program.

And listen, remember what I said earlier that being a Christian doesn't mean we are free of sin. We make mistakes. We fall well short of perfection. Real Christians do not judge others, yet how many times have any of you reading this book judged another human being? How many times have you treated another human being less than graciously? Everyone on this earth is created in the image of God, remember that. Inside of each human being is a God given gift and purpose that needs to manifest and show itself through teaching, coaching, and understanding. We are supposed to help make each other better versions of ourselves by emulating Jesus as much as possible daily. The gospel mandates we change culture and rescue souls.

In May of 2021, I was commissioned as a Colson Fellow during a ceremony in Dallas, Texas. I was very proud to have made it through the program given my full calendar (calendars are not busy, they are full. Busy implies you have no control over it, and you most certainly do). I was also happy with the fact my wife said she was proud of me, as did Rachael. It remains one of my proudest moments to this day.

The darkest moments of my PTSD now seemed like a distance struggle. As I mentioned earlier, spirituality was a key component in my healing. PTSD affects people differently because everyone is wired differently. But knowing what I know now about God, Jesus, and the Holy Spirit, I am convinced if you come to Him and lay your burdens at the cross, He will transform your life. You will realize your purpose. You will gain strength and courage to do what God wants you to do. You will discern His will. You will be a happier, kinder, more generous person.

Don't get me wrong, God doesn't need another nice guy, as John Eldridge says in his book, *Wild at Heart*. He needs a warrior for the kingdom! He needs men and women on fire for Jesus. He needs men and women with a passionate desire to live life to the fullest, as God wants you to live. How many of you know people who give God an hour of their time and only on Sundays? God wants your heart every minute of the day! And it is possible to do so, but you have to give up the ways of this world. Stop focusing on what you want out of life and discern what His will is for your life. Stop idolizing your career or your family even! Yes, it is possible to idolize your spouse. It is possible to idolize your kids. It is possible to idolize sports, movies, alcohol, drugs, and anything at all that you prioritize ahead of God. How many of you take your kids to play sports on Sundays instead of taking them to church? What's more important, playing ball in a fallen world, or learning how to live for eternity in the Kingdom of Heaven? Don't get me wrong, it's not that I believe kids should not play sports, that's not what I am saying. However, certainly not at the expense of attending church and learning about Jesus and how to live life according to Him. Those lessons far exceed the lessons of any sport. Your children will need to learn their biblical purpose in life one day, how are you helping them find it? Have you prioritized anything before God?

My dear friend, Chad LeBoeuf, is a perfect example of how to handle sports on Sundays. He gives his son a choice, attend church on Saturday or before or after his son's soccer game on Sunday. When games are out of town (and they frequently are), Chad actually researches the area where the game is to be held, looking online for nearby church services and their hours. Depending on game time and church service times, they will attend church either before or after the game. This method gives his son an option regarding when to attend church, but attending church itself is never an option. His son knows he will be at church one way or the other. He understands the importance of doing so because his father has made it a priority over soccer. Chad says to his son that playing sports is good, but going to church is a must, it is non-negotiable. How do you prioritize worship services in your life?

When you find your purpose in life, your passion burns bright! But if you do not have a relationship with God, your purpose may take a lifetime to be revealed to you if it is even revealed to you at all. Rachael once shared with me something she once heard that fiercely resonated with her. She said, "They say the two most important days in your life are the day you are born, and the day you realize why." Is that not profound?! If this is true, does it not make sense to realize your purpose in life as quickly as possible so you can devote the rest of it to God's will for you?! Because nothing else matters in eternity, but what you did on earth for the Kingdom of Heaven!

So how then do you go about realizing your purpose in life according to God's design? Well, you must constantly seek to grow closer in your relationship with God. After returning to Christ and going back to church, it still took me almost three years before I had an epiphany, whereas I realized seeking to grow closer to God should be my number one priority above anything else on earth! I realized my relationship with Him should come before my job, my health, before my wife and kids even! Yes, before my family! I quickly found as I grew closer to God, those things in my life which brought me stress, anxiety, or simply challenged me in a difficult way began to fade away! My life began coming into balance for the first time ever.

13

TIO SAM MINISTRIES

> *"The Spirit of the Lord God is upon me, because the Lord has anointed me to bring good news to the poor; he has sent me to bind up the brokenhearted, to proclaim liberty to the captives, and the opening of the prison to those who are bound." – Isaiah 61:1*

WITH MY CHRISTIAN worldview now locked in place, I couldn't help but think about how life would have probably been much easier if I had only given my heart to Jesus much sooner. It is interesting to think about such things, but I also now realize I would not be the man I am today had it not been for those storms I endured. I do live much more peacefully today, even in the storms, than I did before I was saved. The Bible tells us that in this world we will have trouble, and today when I enter into a storm, I do so knowing it will eventually pass, it is merely a season. In the meantime, I ask myself what God is trying to teach me in the midst of storm or what direction is he nudging me. Am I to help a friend or family member, or even a stranger? Am I to refrain from doing something that will not serve me? Am I to do something I may not even realize will serve Him in the end? In these storms, I believe I can make myself that much more receptive to God's word, and He will use me as an instrument of His will if I am obedient. These are the storms that have tempered me and have made me more receptive to His will and teachings.

War, although ugly, does in fact bring with it many opportunities for growth as a human being. The terrors of war have driven men to insanity. In one of my tours, I found myself not just in physical fights for survival, but also in mental fights for my own sanity. The mental fight is what followed me back home. But after making up my mind to follow Christ, declaring my obedience to Him and giving Him my heart, everything changed as you have read. The psychological discomforts of anxiety and loneliness that result from being in combat and not being able to predict the future also followed me home and were also met with the same fate when I gave my heart to Jesus.

You see, the heart is the center of gravity in spiritual warfare. It is all about the heart. This is what the enemy wants, he wants your heart. When you give your heart to Jesus, he returns it pure and sanctified! Isaiah 61:1 outlines the mission of Jesus when he came to this earth! He came here to return our hearts and set us free so we are no longer slaves to sin! If you are no longer a slave to sin, then you are fully alive! And being fully alive brings much glory to God, which is what He wants from us! To be fully alive in Him, to walk with Jesus and carry out your God-given purpose on this earth, not for our own sake, but for His glory!

What is your purpose on this earth? Remember when I told you what Rachael said to me about purpose? The two most important days in a man's life are the day he is born and the day he realizes why. To all of you reading this book, I would argue your purpose is the exact same purpose as mine: to expand the Kingdom of Heaven. It is how we go about it that is different and specific to each individual one of us. Because as people, we are all different, with unique talents and God-given gifts. I can't possibly list every single way one can expand the Kingdom, and I certainly can't tell you what this means for you personally. But I can tell you what it does not mean. It does not mean you settle for a broken, damaged life. It does not mean you resolve yourself to walking around this earth barely making it through life. It does not mean you remain captive to sin! You must break free and live your best life, transforming yourself into the best version of yourself, and leaving a positive impact on this earth while doing so. Zig Ziglar once had this to say about life, "It's not just about the journey, it's about who you become in the process." And you should do all of this not for yourself, but for God, because He commands it!

Men like my good friend Doctor David Tharp helped me realize that the good men who died on the battlefield who were my friends would certainly not want me to live life depressed and with any survivor's guilt or moral injuries. They don't want me moping around with suicidal thoughts. They want me to live life to the max, and for sure not by ending it at my own hands. I can honor all of those who have died in service to our country, even the ones I never knew, by being the best human being I can be. By leaving a positive impact on this world. By helping those in need. By doing what Jesus said we should do, love one another.

I constantly ask God to use me as an instrument of His will. I ask Him daily for guidance and direction, to help me keep Him foremost on my mind in front of all other things. I ask Him to show me how I can best serve Him on any given day. I also ask Him for forgiveness on a daily basis, because I am not perfect. I am a sinner living in a fallen world, but one of the beauties about being saved is that I catch myself when I do sin, and I try to immediately move to correct my behavior or thoughts. I ask Him to hold me accountable. I ask Him to keep me obedient. I ask Him to send me into the fight against evil wherever He needs me. I am a Sheep Dog, I run toward gunfire. I want God to use me as a holy warrior to bring the fight to the enemy.

Like he used Rachael to save me, he used Danette to help me serve others. One day she invited me to join her in getting her towel dirty while volunteering to serve at an event where tons of food was being given away to veterans in need from a non-profit called Soldier's Angels. Their mission, posted on their website, is to provide aid, comfort, and resources to the military, veterans, and their families. Danette had volunteered with them several times before, and on this one occasion I joined her. It was impressive. Long lines of cars formed prior to opening and we prepped and bagged all types of fresh vegetables, boxed food items, milk, and juices. Once the event opened for business, cars would simply pull up to a station and we would load the food into their vehicle for them. I was so humbled to serve my fellow veterans in this way, and I felt a calling to continue serving others in different capacities.

I remember praying that God reveal to me who he wanted me

to serve next. If you recall, I was already serving with Project Healing Heroes, with Strategic Global Commissioning, with my church, with Juice Plus, with the Colson Fellows cohort, and in several other one-off opportunities as well, and I still needed to find time to go to work every day! Well, God speaks to me, not in an auditory manner but through my heart and mind (and sometimes through the people and/or environment around me). In this one instance while praying, I felt God was telling me to create Tio Sam Ministries. I didn't know what that meant. He gave me no other context, none. More about that later.

Another thing I heard God saying to me was for me to clear some things off my plate. He did not say which ones, and He did not say why. He gave me no more context to this either. Well, I was enjoying everything I was a part of. I felt I was helping others in some small capacity here and there. So I shrugged it off as my own mind, or perhaps the enemy whispering in my ear again. Whatever the case, I did not create Tio Sam Ministries and I did not clear anything from my plate, I disobeyed because my own doubts got in the way.

Well, while I was preparing to be commissioned as a Colson Fellow, the curriculum called for me to teach on a topic of my choice, anything I had learned in the program. I was to teach it to an audience of my choice. So, I decided to teach Christian Worldview to teenagers and their parents. I recruited members of my tribe who had teens as well as a few who did not. As I was preparing for this three-day seminar, God once again told me to create Tio Sam Ministries. So, I decided to do it as a means to facilitate my Christian Worldview seminar. In other words, I was able to advertise the course as being brought to folks by Tio Sam Ministries. I had no idea how successful that seminar would become, and I have now facilitated the seminar several times and plan to hopefully bring it to a church near you, either in person or via Zoom! I know many people are tired of Zoom calls, I get it. But that's the best platform I know to facilitate what I do. If you know of a better way, please share! My contact info is at the end of the book.

Tio Sam Ministries will also be an umbrella organization for other plans I have to bring more good into the world. John Stonestreet, President of the Colson Center, likes to ask these four questions that have become my Motivation Monday Mantra:

1. What is good in the world that you can champion?
2. What is evil in the world that you can stop?
3. What is broken in the world that you can restore?
4. What is missing in the world that you can innovate?

These are awesome questions to ask yourself daily, and then step out in faith. For those dealing with PTSD or depression, one can find purpose in these. You can start small then go bigger and bigger as you grow more confidence. These can also force you to step out of your comfort zone as well!

God continued to tell me to make some room on my plate. To let go of some things. I continued to disobey, believing I couldn't possibly be hearing that right. I mean, I was serving in various capacities at that point and while I know it was a lot, I became a master of time management. If something did not appear on the calendar, it did not get done. Whether it was a board meeting or a date with the wife, if it did not appear on my calendar then I was going to miss it. That could mean trouble if we're talking date night!

I did not want to believe God was telling me to stop serving in one of the capacities I was serving in. Then, I met, Tina. Tina lives in my neighborhood and has been collecting donations for the homeless for years. One way she solicits donations is through the neighborhood Facebook group. This is when I first noticed what she was doing. She was taking the donations into San Antonio to homeless people who lived underneath one of the highways. I decided to donate some clothes for her outreach, so we eventually linked up and I learned she was a Christian and on fire for Jesus. It was then she invited me to go with her the next time she went to distribute the donations. I jumped at the chance! She goes every Monday, so the following Monday I met her out there and was immediately struck by the people she had come to know. People who, although homeless and in some cases suffering from mental illness or the effects of hard drugs, were smiling and greatly appreciative for the donated items. Tina would pray with many of them and invited me to pray as well. I was hooked. God moved my heart for this cause and so, Tio Sam Ministries had acquired another mission. Eventually, my church sanctioned the effort as an official outreach, and we go once a month on the last Monday of the month to build God's Kingdom one life at a time. Pretty soon my friend Danette and several other tribe members began helping out, and together we continue to get our towels dirty in this ministry.

Shortly after I started helping the homeless, one of my tribal members and dear friends, Kristan, approached me and asked me if I would help her find some potential locations in the greater San Antonio area for a non-profit she had a friend in called Leaven Kids. They run an after-school mentoring and tutoring program for kids in grades K–5, who are at risk of dropping out of school, joining gangs, or getting involved with drugs and/or alcohol due to residing in low-income housing units.

This is what their website, leavenkids.org, has to say about their mission:

"Leaven Kids shares the love and compassion of Christ through acts of mercy and provides help to our neighbors.

Our mission is to revitalize communities through early education intervention. We live out this mission through practical programs that transform and empower entire communities and the families that call them home.

Leaven Kids is defined as, "a pervasive influence that modifies something or transforms it for the better." We believe that when children are successful in school, and have a positive adult influence in their lives, they are significantly less likely to drop out, commit a crime, or join a gang.

Leaven Kids learning centers are situated in the apartment complexes where our students and their families live. We work to eliminate crime in neighborhoods by providing year-round tutoring and mentoring, as well as a safe place where parents know their children are protected and well cared for."

How could I say no to that?! Kristan and I spent a whole day driving around some of the worst neighborhoods in San Antonio, scouting out potential sites for the Leaven Kids. Kristan would later tell her friends about how when she got in my car that day, I gave her a full briefing on the location of my pistol, extra ammo, and actions on contact (a military term that translates to what we will do in the event we get shot at or are ambushed). Being a retired nurse, she perked up when I told her I had a trauma kit in my backpack located directly behind her seat. Hey, it is just the way I am wired, and since we were going into the potentially hostile territories of some of San Antonio's worst neighborhoods, I felt a contingency brief was in order. Then we did it again when the Executive Director and a few other leaders from the non-profit came for a site survey.

We eventually visited a complex on the east side, where we met an eleven-year-old little boy who told us how gang members would often pay him to grab some of his friends and play in a field near the parking lot, because rival gang members were less likely to conduct a drive-by shooting if kids were in the way. He said it so nonchalantly, as if it was no big deal. I was so moved by this little boy, and the Leaven Kids' staff said this was exactly the type of kid they help with their program.

Before I knew it, the Leaven Kids Executive Director had asked Kristan and I to be on their Strategic Advisory Committee. I did not hesitate to say yes. I love kids, and I remember growing up around gangs, drugs, and violence. This program resonated with me, and I felt God had brought me right to it. I understood now why I needed to clear my plate. I was entering a new season in life, and God had plans for me. So, I finally obeyed and cleared a few things off my plate.

In Genesis, God charges men to work the Garden of Eden and to keep it. As men, we are designed for a biblical purpose that includes being the spiritual headship of our family, loving our wives in a way that sacrifices our own comfort, and providing for our family. When men do not adhere to what God calls us to be as men, our lives begin to crumble all around us. However, when we do carry out this biblical charter, our lives flourish.

Think about it. Think about men who have kids from several women and who are not involved in any of their women's lives. Or how about those who beat their wives and/or their kids, who turn to a life of crime or who are simply absent in their family's life because they are chasing worldly callings? For those men, their family unit suffers, the community suffers, and society suffers. I have seen it all too often, not just in Los Angeles, San Antonio, or Washington D.C., but also in foreign cities all around the world. It is the same story with the same ending. But when men step into that biblical role, you see a family unit thriving in a community that does the same. These are lessons I have learned since being saved.

We cannot allow our PTSD, depression, or pity parties to keep us from doing what God has charged us with. It is bigger than you and me. Our family needs us to provide adequately, our community needs role models, and our society needs servants who are not afraid to step into the fray and leave a lasting impact on this world. Together, we can do exactly that. Because let me tell you something, when you leave this earth, the only true legacy you leave behind will not be the clothes you wore, the big house you lived in, the nice car you drove, or the most expensive material things you owned. It will be the children you raise, the people you served, the example you set for others to follow. That will be your only true legacy. I want to encourage anyone reading this to take the sage advice of my church, and get to seriously know God through service, find freedom through community and positive relationships, discover your true biblical purpose in life and then go out into the world and make a positive difference in someone's life. Steve Jobs once said, "The people who are crazy enough to think they can change the world are the ones who do." Refuse to conform to this world, and instead seek to transform it. May God bless you and yours.

EPILOGUE

I SET out to write this book with the hope it might just save someone's life. In the process, it became incredibly therapeutic, as I called to memory my life's journey to this point in order to write my story. It was an emotional rollercoaster to get through a few of the chapters. However, it was important for me to be as authentic and as vulnerable as possible so that others who are struggling may find me relatable. This is why I went into such painstaking detail when describing some of the tough times, like the day I went to commit suicide. Perhaps it will not only help someone contemplating the unimaginable, but perhaps also the friends and families of such individuals as well.

I started writing this book about three or four years ago, completing only a couple of chapters in those years. I know, I know, that's a painfully slow pace, I got it! But as you have read, I had a full calendar and besides, God's timing is always perfect, right?! So, on January 20th, 2022, a friend and one heck of a leader, U.S. Army Major General Gary Wayne Johnston, (Retired), took his own life only months after retiring. He was a soldier's General, an amazing human being. I first met him when he was the rank of Major, and our paths continued to cross even in combat. His death served as a horrible reminder that the enemy does not discriminate when it comes to suicide. The enemy will whisper in the ear of a young kid and in the ear of a retired senior military officer who had reached the pinnacle of his career, as well as anyone in-between. It lit a fire under me to finish this book.

You have read about what it is I am doing today with my God-given gifts and abilities. None of it is meant to boast, for I give all credit and glory to God. But I want you to see what is possible when you lay everything at His feet. God will use you for the purpose He created you for. This is why I wrote this book. To give people hope. I want you to see how when a man is at the lowest point in his life, God can show up and show off if you'll just turn to Him. If you are dealing with PTSD, I hope this book has given you a way to help you manage that stress. The Triad of Transformation is meant specifically for you and anyone else battling depression and suicide. You can do it. You are not broken. You are not damaged. You are a child of God and are loved beyond measure. Those people around you really do care, just ask them. God does not make junk; you have a purpose. Do NOT let the enemy get the best of you. You are a Sheep Dog, and you need to regain that status and fight back.

I certainly hope you enjoyed reading about my life's journey, but more importantly, I hope it helps even just one person who reads this book. At the end of the day, the government is not going to stop the ever-increasing rate of suicide. Neither the VA nor any non-profit will be able to stop this unprecedented epidemic of veteran suicide. It will take you and your buddies on your left and right flanks, at your twelve o'clock and your six o'clock, to put a serious dent on this problem set. We need to care enough to check in on each other by way of a phone call, a text message, or even a personal visit. Invite your buddy to have a drink or a coffee, breakfast, lunch, or dinner. We also need to be willing to ask the hard question, are you thinking about suicide? Say the word . . . suicide. We need to own it. Moreover, if they say yes, that they are, well, then help them. There are a ton of resources out there, get them some help. However, the best thing you can do is love on them unconditionally and bring them around a tribe that will do the same.

Perhaps some of you reading this are struggling right now. Hang tight. Do NOT give up. The storm will eventually pass, I promise. You are not the first person or the last to deal with whatever issue has you thinking there is no other way. The enemy is counting on that thought. He will encourage it. If you get to that moment, that instant when you are about to do it, just hold on a little bit more, tell yourself to hang on, to stop. The moment will pass. Reach out to someone, anyone you know, for help. Suicide is not the right answer for anything.

May God bless all of you.

ABOUT THE AUTHOR

Mr. Sammy Villela, a.k.a. "Tio Sam," is a U.S. Army Veteran and currently a Counterintelligence Special Agent in the Department of Defense with over thirty-two years of experience chasing terrorists and spies in the U.S. and hot spots around the globe, including in both Operations Iraqi Freedom and Enduring Freedom in Iraq and Afghanistan respectively. He has published articles in military journals and periodicals on leadership and intelligence topics.

Sammy is on the Board of Directors for Project Healing Heroes, an organization dedicated to helping Veterans battle the invisible wounds of war.

Commissioned as a Colson Fellow, Sammy previously served as the Co-Director of the San Antonio Colson Fellows Cohort. He founded Tio Sam Ministries in order to educate teenagers on how to maintain a biblical worldview despite the subtle influences of our culture today. Sammy also co-founded Strategic Global Commissioning, a non-profit organization providing risk information and liaison services to Christian missionaries. Sammy is currently the Director of Safety at Revolution Church, a health and wellness advocate with Juice Plus (a nutrition company inspiring healthy living around the world), and a member of The

Leaven Kids' Strategic Advisory Committee in San Antonio, Texas.

A native of Texas, Sammy is on a mission to start a revolution of grace in one life at a time! Sammy has been invited to share his testimony at various high schools, universities, churches, and other venues throughout the country and has been featured in numerous media outlets to include San Antonio's 'Street Talk Entertainment Magazine,' KENS 5 News, IMPACT - Stories of Faith AM 630 'The Word,' the Healthy Warriors of Faith Podcast, The Pursuit Podcast, and the Military Officers Association of America Podcast. Sammy was also featured on Grunt Style's *American Grit* show where he was coined as "Cibolo's Favorite Son" by the show's host.

Sammy advocates for a faith-based, principle-centered philosophy for a purposeful life that encourages one to seriously get to know God through service, find freedom through community and positive relationships, discover one's true biblical purpose in life, and then go out into the world and make a positive difference! Sammy is convicted in his beliefs we all came here not to conform to the world, but to transform it!

Sammy is married to his lovely wife, Tricia, and together they have four sons, a daughter-in-law, and two grandkids. Along with his parents and younger brother, the Villela Clan all currently reside in the greater area of San Antonio, Texas.

CONNECT WITH SAMMY!

(scan the QR code)

Sammy & Tricia's Wedding Day

Sammy and wife, Tricia celebrating their 25th anniversary

PHOTO ALBUM

Sammy loving on his wife!

Serving in Iraq

Flying over Aghanistan

PHOTO ALBUM

Searching for bad guys

At Red Square in Moscow, Russia

PHOTO ALBUM

FBI Director, Christopher Wray, and Sammy

The famous car ride where Rachael (left) invites Sammy to church. Jacqi in the backseat.

PHOTO ALBUM

Rachael, Sammy & Danette at Hymns n Hops!

Sammy & Rachael

PHOTO ALBUM

Guest Speaker at Redeeming Grace Church, Converse, TX

5K fundraiser for Project Healing Heroes d.b.a. CombatPTSD.org

PHOTO ALBUM

Newspaper article that ran when Sammy signed up to be a counterspy

The Villela Family. From left to right, back row: Victor, Adam, Jesse, Alex. Front row: Sammy and Tricia.

Made in the USA
Coppell, TX
18 June 2022